THE
FINANCIAL SECTOR
OF THE AMERICAN
ECONOMY

edited by
STUART BRUCHEY
University of Maine

A GARLAND SERIES

RISKS AND REPORTING OF OFF-BALANCE-SHEET (OBS) ACTIVITIES IN COMMERCIAL BANKING

REBA LOVE CUNNINGHAM

GARLAND PUBLISHING, INC.
NEW YORK & LONDON / 1994

Library of Congress Cataloging-in-Publication Data

Cunningham, Reba Love, 1939–
    Risks and reporting of off-balance-sheet (OBS) activities in commercial
banking / Reba Love Cunningham.
        p.   cm. — (The Financial sector of the American economy)
    Includes bibliographical references and index.
    ISBN 0–8153–1743–3 (alk. paper)
    1. Banks and banking—United States—Accounting.   2. Financial
statements—United States.   3. Disclosure in accounting—United
States.   I. Title. II. Title: Off-balance-sheet activity.   III. Series.
HG1708.C86   1994
657'.8333—dc20   93–47530
                                                           CIP

HG1708
.C86
1994

Printed on acid-free, 250-year-life paper
Manufactured in the United States of America

Contents

Tables

Preface

A review of the current business literature reveals that off-balance-sheet (OBS) activities remain an active issue. Financial theorists, those in the financial services industry, regulators and accounting policy makers continue to explore the reasons for and impact of the use of OBS financial instruments. The principal items examined in both the theoretical and empirical literature are standby letters of credit, loan commitments, loan sales, and interest rate swaps [Hassan 1993]. The empirical investigation reported upon in this book centers on three of these--standby letters of credit, loan sales, and interest rate swaps--as well as commercial letters of credit.

Two important events referred to as future events in the book have now occurred. These are the requirement by the Federal Deposit Insurance Corporation (FDIC) that commercial banks include certain OBS items in their computation of regulatory capital. In addition, the Financial Accounting Standards Board (FASB) issued Financial Accounting Standard No.105 which requires certain disclosure regarding OBS activity. The specific requirements of each of these are explained in the chapter two of the book. Some empirical analyses of the changes resulting from risk-based capital have been published. Thus far, no study has investigated the impact of FAS No. 105 upon OBS activity.

The recently published articles in the OBS activity area are of two basic types. The first category is analytical analyses of how the financial instrument works and its theoretical underpinnings. This type of article is particularly prevalent in the interest rate swaps literature. Wall[1989] attempts to reconcile claims that interest rate swap financing reduces financing costs through "comparative advantage" with the academic argument which questions the existence of a "comparative advantage". His findings suggest that short-term debt combined with interest rate swaps may reduce financing costs by allowing firms with high risk to reduce agency costs without incurring interest rate risk. Wall's study offers possible avenues of empirical study, but Wall does not perform any empirical investigation. Richard Filler [1993] wrote an article describing how basic interest rate swaps work. His work supplies nothing new since it simply outlines some of the risks and hidden costs associated with interest rate swaps. A more theoretical explanation for the existence of interest rate swaps is provided by Arak, Estrella, Goodman, and Silver [1988]. These authors, all associated with commercial banking, present their model of how interest rate swaps behave. They conclude that borrowers who are pessimistic about future risk-free interest rates, but optimistic about their own credit standing find that borrowing in the short-term market and swapping into fixed-rate payments provides the preferred financing mechanisms. Smith, Smithson, and Wakeman [1988] assert that the argument that arbitrage of quality spreads explains the enormous growth of interest rate swaps is unsatisfying. Instead, they believe that the growth of the swap market has resulted from reductions in the bid/ask spread, an increase in the demand for risk management instruments, and the ability to use swaps to create synthetic financial instruments. Smith, et al [1988] arrive at two conclusions. First, the default risk for an interest rate swap is determined by the credit rating of the contracting firm, correlation between the contracting firm's value and interest rates, the volatility of interest rates, the term structure's slope, the maturity of the swap, the frequency of the difference checks, and whether some performance bond is posted. Second, Smithson, et al [1988] state that cash flow implications of default for a portfolio of swaps are significantly different than those of a single contract. Their analyses supports the idea that default risk faced by a bank in the interest rate swap market should be manageable through portfolio diversification.

Vang [1993] reported the results of an empirical investigation of the role of interest rate swaps in savings and loan associations. Vang uses am empirical model of the relationship between equity and swaps in the savings and loan industry. Quarterly data from fifty-three firms for the period beginning 1986 and continuing through the middle quarter of 1987 provided the data base for Vang's research. Vang's study supports a positive relationship between capital and swap usage. This result agrees to the relationship between OBS instrument activity and capital found in commercial banking and adds support to that relationship. Zimmer [1991] tests a model constructed to simulate default patterns of interest rate swaps. The estimated models exhibit good predictive power, particularly with regard to forecasting major upswings in credit risk. Zimmer also attempts to evaluate interest rate risk and currency swaps using arbitrage models.

A number of authors examine the risk/return relationship in commercial banks. These are the studies by Eberle [1991], Brewer [1992], and Khambata [1989]. Each of these researchers use empirical data to test the relationship between the use of OBS financial instruments and risk to the financial institution.

Two reported studies investigate the risk-based capital framework, its application, and impact. The studies include Charlton [1991], and Millard [1989]. Millard's paper concentrates upon an investigation of the requirement of reporting of OBS instruments on risk-based capital. Charlton's discussion centers upon the pricing effect of risk-based capital regulations. Millard's work analyzes the requirements of risk-based capital. Millard appears to support the idea that risk-based capital is a necessary first step in maintaining capital adequacy.

Standby letters of credit still command the distinction of being the single most reported upon OBS financial instrument. Articles or dissertations reviewed by this author include Quinn [1992], Charlton [1991], Koppenhaver [1991], and Pawlowic [1991]. Quinn's [1992] research supports the idea that using standby letters of credit in lieu of conventional letters of credit may result in reduced costs by users. Charlton [1991] presents a model that focusses management on meeting return on equity goals while bringing into consideration the basic overhead costs and the costs of credit quality. This model provides the reader with a reasonable mechanism for estimating pricing of standby letters of credit and letters of credit. Koppenhaver's [1991] article examines the relationship between the issuance of standby letters of credit and capital of the commercial bank. Pawlowic [1991] writes a review and update of the external factors such as changes in the Uniform Commercial Code and the advent of risk-based capital.

Several articles on loan sales have entered the recent business literature. Thomas [1991] uses an event test methodology to demonstrate the benefits of loan sales to the existing debtholders. A wealth transfer from the shareholders to debtholders is also shown to exist. This implies a decrease in the default risk of the issuing firm. Both results are consistent with the collateralization hypothesis. Vrabel [1989] provides an analysis of securitization of assets which can be used in formulating bank policy. Schauer [1991] rejects the hypothesis that buyers' or sellers' portfolios are weakened by loan sales. Further, this author concludes that banks primary motivation for selling loans is not to avoid regulatory taxes. Rather, the assertion is that loan sales are a natural evolutionary process of the short-term credit market. Hassan [1993] shows that loan sales are priced as risk-reducing by investors, not risk-increasing. Toolan [1991] discusses the advantages of standard documentation of loan sales. An empirical investigation by Wall [1991] suggests that providing recourse in loan sales may not increase risks when indirect effects of recourse through loan purchaser monitoring are taken into account. Pruden [1990] discusses changing provisions in loan agreements and their economic consequences.

Finally, a review of the positive accounting theory (PAT) reveals that PAT, always a controversial subject, is subjected to heavy criticism. Sterling [1990], Williams [1989], and Boland and Gordon [1992] each find little to recommend the Watts and Zimmerman theory.

In summary, material continues to be published on OBS financial instruments. None of the articles or dissertations duplicate this study. It remains unique because of the methodology employed and its database used. While certain articles lend validity to this book, none contradicts or discredits this information.

Risks and Reporting of Off-Balance-Sheet (OBS) Activities in Commercial Banking

I

Introduction

The use of innovative financial instruments, which may be subject to off-balance-sheet (OBS) risk, presents a threat to the integrity of financial reporting. The Financial Accounting Standards Board (FASB) in its Concepts Statement No. 1 *Objectives of Financial Reporting by Business Enterprises* [1986] states that "the objectives for financial reporting for business enterprises are based on the need to provide information that is useful to present and potential investors and creditors and other users in making rational investment, credit, and similar decisions about a particular enterprise."

Some financial instruments, such as interest rate swaps, most options, and interest rate forwards transactions had few specific accounting requirements prior to Statement of Financial Accounting Standards (SFAS) No. 105. The use of these instruments was neither reported nor disclosed in the financial statements, yet these transactions carry inherent risk to the participating enterprise [Stewart 1989]. Present and potential investors cannot accurately assess the financial integrity of an enterprise without full information as to its credit risk, market risk, and liquidity risk. Current accounting recognition and disclosure requirements may not provide adequate guidance to assure that sufficient information about OBS activities is made available to present and potential investors. The disclosure requirements of SFAS No. 105 may alleviate some of this information inadequacy.

Companies using OBS instruments may have liabilities and cash flow requirements which are not adequately disclosed; data may be buried within footnotes or in the management's discussion and analysis section of the annual report. The failure to include these obligations in financial statements may lead readers to understate or overstate liabilities, understate cash flow requirements, and compute misleading financial ratios.

Financial institutions, particularly commercial banks, may be engaging in OBS activity without realistically assessing the associated risks to the firm. Banks' managements may be making poor long-run investment choices because of accounting and disclosure considerations.

PURPOSE OF THE RESEARCH

The primary purpose of this research is to develop a model of common characteristics of banks that participate in the OBS market. Knowledge of these characteristics should be helpful to present and potential investors, auditors, and regulators. The study is designed to determine if a link exists between the characteristics of participants and the accounting choices of bank management.

SCOPE OF THE RESEARCH

The present study is exploratory and is limited to commercial banks and four selected financial instruments: standby letters of credit (SLCs), commercial letters of credit (LOCs,) interest rate swaps (SWAPs), and loan sales (SALEs). The research develops a predictive model of common characteristics of commercial banks that use SLCs, LOCs, interest rate swaps, and loan sales. Financial institutions, defined here as commercial banks, are examined because these firms have participated most actively in the OBS financial instruments market. Banks also have explicit disclosure requirements for these instruments on their Consolidated Asset and Liability (CALL) reports. These reports are submitted quarterly to the Federal Deposit Insurance Corporation (FDIC) and Federal Reserve System (FED).

The banks' involvement in OBS transactions will be identified from information found in Schedules L and M of each bank's CALL report.These schedules require that banks list their commitments and contingencies. Specific disclosure requirements of Schedule L [Federal Banking Law Reporter, 1990] for the four selected financial instruments are the dollar volume of:
  I.   Standby letters of credit and foreign office guarantees
       1.To U.S. addressees
       2.To non U.S. addressees
       3.Amount of standby letters of credit in items
       (1) and (2) conveyed to others
  II. Commercial and similar letters of credit

III. Loans originated by the reporting bank that have been sold or participated to others during the reporting period
IV. Notional value of all outstanding interest rate swaps.

Schedule L of the CALL reports of the banks provided financial data to compute the dependent variables used in the study. Dependent variables are a ratio of each of the four financial instruments-SLCs, LOCs, interest rate swaps, and loan sales-to earning assets of the bank. Financial data to compute the independent variables, except for percentage of stock held by directors and officers as a group, is from the income statement, balance sheet, and other related schedules of the CALL report. Independent variables include: (1) earnings growth, (2) return on assets, (3) dividend payout, (4) return on equity, (5) net interest income, (6) non-interest income, (7) primary capital ratio, (8) total capital ratio, (9) equity capital ratio, (10) equity capital ratio less minimum required capital ratio, (11) size, (12) debt/equity ratio, (13) percentage of stock held by directors and officers as a group, (14) loan loss reserve ratio, (15) demand deposits/total liabilities, (16) cash ratio, (17) interest-bearing cash ratio, (18) federal funds sold ratio, (19) unpledged securities ratio, (20) quick ratio, and (21) current ratio. These variables and rationale for their inclusion are further described in Chapter Five. The general research question of the study is:

Are there financial characteristics of the firm such as its profitability measures, regulatory measures, agency issues, and liquidity measures which predict managements' decision to use OBS financial instruments?

Specific hypotheses were developed from the research question. To test the hypotheses regression models were developed from the independent and dependent variables named.

The association between changes in the independent variables and any change in the firm's activity in an OBS financial instrument is of particular interest. An ordinary least squares (OLS) regression analysis procedure is used to analyze the data. Because of multicollinearity problems, factor analysis followed by regression of the factors is used to analyze the data in addition to the OLS regression procedure.

ORGANIZATION OF THE BOOK

Chapter Two presents descriptive information about the structure and economics of transactions involving each type of financial instrument being investigated. These instruments are SLCs, LOCs, interest rate swaps, and loan sales. The inherent risks in using these OBS financial instruments are discussed. A brief description of existing accounting and/or disclosure requirements pertaining to SLCs, LOCs, interest rate swaps, and loan sales is included.

Chapter Three provides a review of the prior research in the OBS area. This review includes summaries and analyses of studies investigating the economic consequences of OBS transactions, selected portions of the work in the positive theory of accounting choice, and studies examining specific aspects of the SLCs, LOCs, interest rate swaps, and loan sales.

Chapter Four sets forth the theoretical framework of the research. The question arises as to the applicability of the positive theory of accounting choice to the decision to participate in the OBS market.

Chapter Five outlines the methodology used to empirically test the hypotheses. A description of the variables along with the expected association between independent and dependent variables is included.

Data analysis and interpretation is presented in Chapter Six. Conclusions drawn from the results are discussed.

The final chapter provides a listing of this study's contributions to the body of accounting literature. Implications of the study to investors, auditors, accounting policy setters, and regulators are described. Limitations of the present research and suggestions for future research are also presented.

II

Economics, Risks, and Accounting for Standby Letters of Credit, Letters of Credit, Interest Rate Swaps and Loan Sales

Descriptions and examples of the financial instruments included in the study, standby letters of credit (SLCs), commercial letters of credit (LOCs), interest rate swaps (SWAPs), and loan sales (SALEs) are provided. The descriptions illustrate the difficulties faced by third party users of financial statements when a firm uses off balance sheet (OBS) financial instruments. Accounting and/or disclosure requirements are also briefly discussed. Tables 10 through 13 in Appendix A present examples of each of these transactions to help the reader understand each instrument.

STANDBY LETTERS OF CREDIT

There are typically three parties to a SLC transaction: the bank (issuer), the bank's customer (the account party), and a third party (the beneficiary) [Goldberg and Lloyd-Davies 1985]. Usually SLCs arise when the account party and beneficiary enter into a contract which creates an obligation of the account party to the beneficiary.

About 60 percent of current standby letters of credit (SLCs) are financial guarantees. These instruments require the bank to guarantee the financial obligation of a borrower to a specified third party [Andrews and Sender 1986]. SLCs are bankers' riskiest item because activation of a SLC results in an immediately questionable loan [Andrews and Sender 1986].

7

Economics of SLC Transactions

The purpose of a SLC is to ensure to the beneficiary that the contract will be fulfilled; or if it is not, the bank will make a cash settlement to the beneficiary. Normally SLCs expire unused because the account party performs under the contract terms. To illustrate a typical SLC, assume that the account party wishes to issue commercial paper or bonds and to reduce interest cost through "credit enhancement." Obtaining a SLC from a bank that has a credit rating superior to its own increases the account party's credit rating and lowers the interest cost. In effect, the bank's creditworthiness is substituted for the account party's. The bank receives a fee for making the commitment, but the bank is not required to use any of its assets unless the account party defaults. See table 10 in Appendix A for an illustration.

Risks

Risk involved in standby letters of credit include market risk, credit risk, liquidity risk, underpricing risk, and systematic risk. Each of these risks are defined and discussed.

Market risk is, perhaps, the most volatile. A frequent application of SLC 'credit enhancement' is providing liquidity assurances for variable rate municipal issues [Koppenhaver 1987]. Market risk for the issuing bank illustrated by this transaction arises when an unexpected disequilibrium condition in the municipal market activates numerous standby letters of credit thus concentrating credit exposure of the banks in one industry. For example, a default by a major issuer in the municipal market could initiate a significant numbers of calls on liquidity guarantees made by a bank. A dramatic rise in interest rates above the caps on most variable-rate municipal issues could create a similar problem [Andrews and Sender 1986]. Banks are obligated by their SLC agreements to buy and hold the bonds put by investors until the issuer can repurchase them. If a number of issuers were short of cash, some banks could end up holding these bonds for lengthy periods. The banks would have numerous borrowers unable to pay the market rate of interest to which banks are entitled. Because of these market forces, liquidity guarantees of a client's financial paper may carry exposure despite the financial integrity of the client. (Default risk is the risk associated with a client's financial integrity). The market and interest rate risk associated with the financial instruments issued by the client accrue to the bank.

Most bank managers [Ernst & Whinney 1986] underplay the credit risk of standbys. Credit risk is that risk associated with making a loan, i.e., the client's ability to repay the loan. The majority of bank managers assessed SLC risk as moderate or standard because the bank applies the same credit risk evaluations to SLCs as to regular loans. However, despite sophistication of a bank's credit analysis, the financial soundness of the transaction may be overrated. Historically, however, the numbers support the bankers' positions. Only about two percent of all standby letters of credit are known to have been called by bank customers [Goldberg and Lloyd-Davies 1985]. Losses averaged an insignificant .77 percent on loans resulting from SLCs in 1984. Since the Goldberg and Lloyd-Davies [1985] study, volume of SLCs issued has steadily increased. SLCs outstanding grew from $80.8 billion in June 1982 to $153.2 billion in June 1985-a 90 percent increase [Bennett 1986]. SLC activity of the sampled banks increased from a mean of $293,331,000 in 1987 to $354,267,000 in 1988.

However, the expanded use of SLCs may be changing the overall risk. The Goldberg and Lloyd-Davies [1985] study cited in Chapter Three showed that capital markets penalize bank money market liabilities by demanding additional premium when the issuing banks increase their risky assets relative to capital. However, Goldberg and Davies' could not specifically attribute the increase in risk premium to the use of SLCs. The failure of Penn Square National Bank in 1982 provided supporting evidence that SLCs may significantly increase overall bank risk. Penn Square's ratio of SLCs to capital (net of participations) was in excess of 200 percent immediately prior to its failure [Goldberg and Lloyd-Davies 1985]. Whether or not this is an anomaly or a significant relationship is an empirical question. The common characteristics of banks heavily using SLCs identified by the research provides some insight into this issue.

Banks bear a liquidity risk associated with SLCs because of the potential impact upon their own portfolios. Suppose at a time when the bank has insufficient cash to fund the guarantee, an SLC is activated. The bank must liquidate assets to provide cash. The bank could be forced to incur losses on its own portfolio in order to cover the guarantee or to hold assets in less productive investments. Bankers are understandably reluctant to release information on actual loss occurrences. The question is an empirical one, as yet unreported.

Another form of risk associated with SLCs is the bank-specific risk of underpricing the guarantee [Koppenhaver 1987]. The fee associated with issuing an SLC is a function of the market's perception of the difference in the creditworthiness of the account party (the bank's customer) and the issuer (the bank) as well as the demand for SLCs. Fees charged to the bank's customers to open the credit line may be thought of as a premium on an insurance policy. The maximum the bank can charge is the present value of all default risk premium payments that the direct financing market would charge in the absence of the SLC. There are three valid reasons that the initial fees can be less than the market's default risk premium. These are (1) a strong bank-client relationship is promoted, (2) the bank has better information about the client's financial integrity than the market, and (3) savings in regulatory taxes reduce the effective cost of bearing the risk. Underestimating the present value of the default risk premium or overestimating the reasons of reducing the fee (which is far more likely) can result in underpricing the fee charged for the SLC relative to the risk assumed [Koppenhaver 1987].

A link between guarantee issuance and systematic risk also exists [Koppenhaver 1987]. The Option Pricing Model can be used to show that a firm's liabilities has systematic risk that varies in direct proportion to the systematic risk of the firm's assets. Guarantees are a contingent liability. The bank, in essence, writes a put option for the standby beneficiary. This conveys the right to sell the borrower's liability to the bank over the life of the commitment. If bank liabilities are options with systematic risk related to the value of the bank, SLCs have systematic risk related to the value of the bank. There is more discussion of this relationship in Chapter Three.

Accounting and Disclosure

Statement of Financial Accounting Standard (FAS) No. 5 [FASB 1990] requires disclosure of a guarantee. The disclosure provisions of the Statement apply to SLCs even though the probability of loss may be remote, because SLCs are guarantees. However, SFAS No. 5 does not specify details of what facts of SLC transactions should be disclosed. During the time of this study a wide disparity of information included in external financial reports existed. Most banks did not reveal concentration of credit risk by industry or customer, average original maturities, or average remaining maturities. Banks generally reported required disclosure as specified by SFAS No. 105 and Accounting Principles Board (APB) Opinion No. 22. Disclosure included information concerning the contract amount of the SLC. In addition, a discussion of the credit and market risk of the instruments, cash requirements, and related accounting policies pursuant to Accounting Principles Board (APB) Opinion No. 22 are required.

Regulatory reporting requirements for SLCs have been effective for several years. In response to the failure of the United States National Bank of San Diego in 1973, federal banking authorities required banks to disclose SLCs in their CALL reports and their annual reports [Cates and Davis 1987]. The failure was, in part, attributed to United States National's using SLCs to back loans made by other financial institutions to companies controlled by the bank's principal stockholder. At that time this was the largest bank failure in United States banking history.

SLC Summary

The growth in issuance of SLCs reflects the increased demand for financial guarantees. The pool of borrowers available to banks has changed because more and more high-quality borrowers are relying on direct financing. Banks are asked to provide guarantees via SLCs to borrowers with poorer credit ratings. The loss of traditional loans results in a loss of traditional revenue, i.e., interest income. Banks seek alternative sources of income. SLCs provide a source of fee income for commercial banks.

Since the bank is called upon to activate an SLC only in the event of some type of financial distress by the client, an immediately troublesome loan results. The combination of the probability of questionable loans plus the enormous volume of absolute dollars potentially committed through SLCs may represent a greater overall risk than traditional bank loans.

COMMERCIAL LETTERS OF CREDIT

A commercial letter of credit is a formal document issued by a buyer's bank substituting the bank's creditworthiness for the buyers'. The LOC is payable upon presentation of certain documents. The letters are for specified amounts and periods of time. Commercial letters of credit are generally used to finance the movement or storage of goods and are normally payable by a bank after it receives documentation that title to the goods has been conveyed [Goldberg and Lloyd-Davies 1985]. The traditional LOC was developed over hundreds of years of international commerce to aid in trade between buyers and sellers unfamiliar with each other [Verkuil 1973]. Historically, the bulk of imports has been financed by letters of credit. The convenience, reliability, and inexpensiveness of the LOC has encouraged its expanded use [Verkuil 1973]. The parties and documentation required for a typical LOC are illustrated on Table 11 in Appendix A.

Economics of LOCs

A seller may not be willing to extend credit to an unknown customer. A buyer made not have sufficient funds or the desire to pay for goods prior to their delivery. The bank letter of credit bridges this gap. A buyer arranges for a bank, whose credit is acceptable to the seller, to issue a LOC. In the LOC the bank agrees to pay drafts drawn on it by the seller, if and only if, certain specified documents such as bills of lading or air freight receipts, accompany the draft. The documents represent title to the goods that are the subject of the transaction. The bank undertakes this obligation for a specified period of time. Documentation follows specific guidelines. The Comptroller of the Currency in Interpretive Ruling No. 7-7916 [1972] delineates the required elements of a LOC.[1]

Letters of credit must meet certain transactional needs. The seller wants contract fulfillment, convenience, prompt payment, and advice. The assurances that an issuing bank provides the seller are that the contract will be paid in full within a specified time period. The LOC also ensures the seller that funds will be received at the seller's own bank or a bank of the seller's country. The LOC also assures the seller

---

[1]The five elements of a LOC are (1) the bank must receive a fee, (2) the LOC must have a specified term, (3) the LOC must have a maximum amount, (4) the bank's obligation to pay must arise only upon presentation of specific documents, and (5) the bank's customer must have an unqualified obligation to reimburse the bank in the same condition as the bank has paid.

that the contract will be paid in full within a specified time. Payment is promptly made upon the sale of the goods. The use of a LOC also facilitates complex trade transactions by providing personnel knowledgeable in international trade and the use of LOCs to the seller. The issuing bank provides the buyer documentary expertise in making payment, managing cash flow, and expert assistance in dealing with the specific procedures necessary to negotiate a complex LOC transaction.

Risks

LOC transactions carry two basic risks for issuing banks-normal credit risk and documentary risk [Verkuil 1973]. Credit exposure tends not to be as well controlled for LOCs as traditional lending [Cates and Davis 1987]. When a bank disburses funds to honor a LOC, it anticipates a quick reimbursement by the customer. Because of the expected quick turnaround, bankers discount the likelihood of default by the customer and tend not to manage this credit in the same way as traditional loans. That is, LOCs tend not to be controlled, as traditional loans are, by a conscientious and experienced loan officer operating under a well-defined loan agreement [Cates and Davis 1987]. Such relaxed credit increases the likelihood of making an imprudent loan. Further, there is less likelihood of working out a satisfactory repayment scheme in the event of default by the buyer [Cates and Davis 1987].

The second risk is documentary risk [Verkuil 1973]. The issuing bank gives the seller assurance that a stated sum of money will be paid at sight or within a prescribed time limit upon receipt of certain stipulated documents. The bank pays the overseas advising bank, the exporter's bank. Later the opening party, the importer, may discover a discrepancy in the documents and refuse to pay the bank. Payment is based on documents only, not on merchandise or services involved.

Investors and regulators generally believe that, because of their nature, LOCs do not bear the same risk as SLCs. However, currently no loss record for LOCs is disclosed. Income statements for banks fail to show the fees received for these products as separately identifiable amounts. Information for appropriate risk-return assessment is not available in banks' annual reports.

Accounting and Disclosure

Commercial letters of credit are omitted from the requirements of SFAS No. 5. Nevertheless, LOCs do carry credit risks for the issuer. Fees from LOCs are included in non-interest income as service charges; this aggregation of income from several sources obscures the amount earned in relation to the risk taken. Third-party users of financial statements have little information to evaluate a risk-return tradeoff for LOCs. A model of common characteristics of banks that issue large volumes of LOCs may be helpful in alerting readers of financial statements of potential undisclosed risks.

SFAS No. 105 [FASB 1990] does not specifically mention LOCs. However, the definition of financial instrument clearly encompasses LOCs, and the statement does not specifically exclude LOCs. Disclosure requirements for *all* financial instruments with off-balance-sheet risk include the face, contract, or notional principal amount. The nature of terms of the contract must be revealed. Credit and market risk of the instruments, cash requirements, and related accounting policies must be discussed. (These requirements are not new.) The firm should disclose the amount of accounting loss that would be incurred if any party to the financial instrument failed to perform completely. The bank's disclosure requirements include its policy regarding requiring collateral or other security, the nature and a brief description of the collateral, and the entity's access to the collateral. The Statement also requires disclosure of information about significant concentrations of credit risk from an opening party or groups of opening parties [FASB 1990].

LOC Summary

Commercial letters of credit are financial guarantees used primarily in international commerce. The issuing bank substitutes its own credit for that of the buyer. The LOC meets certain needs of the buyer and the seller. The seller wants contract fulfillment, convenience, prompt payment, and advice. The buyer wants contract fulfillment, convenience, credit and expert advice. The intermediating bank satisfies both needs.

Issuing banks experience normal credit risk and documentary risk with LOCs. Generally these risks are not considered as great as the risks associated with SLCs. However, current disclosure requirements do not provide sufficient information to assess a risk-return tradeoff with LOCs. The disclosure requirements of SFAS No. 105 apply, but fees earned from LOCs is not a line item on the income statement. The risk/return evaluation cannot be determined from publicly available information.

INTEREST RATE SWAPS

An interest rate swap is a financial transaction in which a series of interest payments are exchanged without exchanging the underlying debt. See Table 12 in Appendix A for an example of a basic swap transaction. Interest rate swaps have grown at an astounding rate during the 1980s to become one of the most popular devices used to hedge interest rate risk [Bicksler and Chen 1986]. Dollar volume increased from under $10 million in 1981 to an amount in excess of $100 billion in 1985 [Lereah 1986]. Merrill Lynch indicated that its swap volume grew in 1986 from $220 million per month in January to $2 billion per month in August [Wall Street Journal 1986]. SWAP activity for the sampled banks peaked at a maximum per bank of $22,413,601,000 in 1988.

Economics of Swap Transactions

Interest rate swaps are voluntary and are based on the notion that each party receives an economic benefit from the transaction. Whittaker [1987] identifies some of the reasons for swaps. One such reason is the firm's ability to reduce borrowing costs through financial arbitrage. These opportunities for arbitrage exist when borrowing costs for the same borrowers differ in the various credit markets. Bondholders are concerned with credit quality because they are lending for extended periods of time at a fixed rate. The yield on fixed-rate bonds usually includes a large risk premium for bonds issued by firms that are perceived to have a high default risk. The risk premium for the same firms is usually less for floating rate bonds because lenders have the opportunity to adjust the lending rate. A firm with a lower credit rating has a comparative advantage in the short-term floating-rate market. A firm with a higher credit rating may have a comparative advantage in raising long-term fixed-rate debt. The highly creditworthy company can issue floating-rate bonds in conjunction with an interest rate swap and lower its cost. The lower-rated firm must pay larger premiums for borrowing in the bond market, but it can use a swap to lower that cost by borrowing short-term floating rate funds and swapping for the fixed-rate payments of the better-rated firm. See Appendix A for an illustration of the mechanics of a swap.

Interest rate swaps also can be used as a gap management tool, i.e., a hedge against interest rate risk [Whittaker 1987]. Gap is a measure of the general interest rate risk faced by banks and is a function of the difference between risk sensitive assets and risk sensitive liabilities. Financial institutions with traditionally fixed-rate mortgage loans have a maturity mismatch with their short-term deposits. These institutions can swap their floating-rate interest payments on short-term deposits for fixed interest payments; or they can swap its fixed-rate income on loans for floating-rate interest income. By doing so, the financial institution better matches the income stream on its assets to the payment stream on its liabilities. This reduces the risk of a capital loss due to unexpected increases in interest rates. Interest rate increases lower the market price of the financial instrument.

Another use of interest rate swaps is to restructure the debt mix of a firm [Bicksler and Chen 1986]. Managers may perceive that the entity has too much in high-coupon fixed-rate liabilities outstanding and use a swap as a liability management tool. The firm could issue floating-rate liabilities and use the proceeds to buy back the existing high-coupon fixed-rate debt. Alternatively, a rate swap can be used to achieve the same goal. The following example illustrates this swap.

* A firm has $50 million of noncallable debt outstanding
* the debt carries a fixed interest rate of 14%
* the debt matures in five years
* The company enters into an interest rate swap with the following terms:
  a. it agrees to pay the prime rate (assume 9.5%) plus 50 basis points
  b. it will receive 13% from the fixed-rate payer in return

The interest rate swap results in a net floating-rate cost of 11 percent. Through the swap the company has converted its high-cost fixed-rate corporate debt into a cheaper floating-rate liability. Swaps are also used to manage basis risk [Bicksler and Chen 1986]. Under a floating\floating interest rate swap, both parties pay floating rates of interest based on different floating rate indices. The following example illustrates this type of swap.

* A bank has an asset which yields a return of the London Interbank Offered Rate (LIBOR) plus .75 percent.
* The asset has been financed with a floating-rate certificate of deposit (CD) at Treasury-bill rate minus .25 percent.
* The counterparty has floating-rate funds at 25 percent above the LIBOR rate.
* The bank pays to the counterparty floating-rate interest equal to the LIBOR rate (reset every six months).
* The bank receives from the counterparty floating-rate interest equal to the T-Bill rate plus .50 percent (reset weekly).

The economic implication of this transaction is that the bank has changed its T-Bill rate-based CD liability into a liability with a cost .75 percent below the LIBOR rate and has locked in a positive spread of 150 basis points against its LIBOR-rate-based assets. The effective cost of the floating rate funds to the counterparty after the swap transaction is equal to the T-Bill rate plus .75 percent.

Participants in the swap market include end-users and intermediaries [Whittaker 1987]. Banks are both end-users and intermediaries. End-users are those who want to swap contractual interest payment streams for a different type of payment stream. Intermediaries arrange the swaps, collect and disburse payments that are swapped, and assume the risk of default by end-users.

The role of commercial banks as intermediaries has increased in the 1980s [Whittaker 1987]. Intermediaries now keep inventories of standardized swaps available to end-users upon request. This practice is called "warehousing" of swaps. The intermediary enters into swaps with end-users before finding an off-setting swap with another end-user. These intermediaries play the role of dealer to increase the liquidity of the swap market and make it more convenient for end-users to arrange swaps.

Opinions differ about the reasons for the existence of the swap market. Bicksler and Chen [1986] argue the economic justification for swaps lies in the arbitrage opportunity offered. Institutional differences imply the presence of market imperfections and the presence of comparative advantages among different borrowers in the market, which creates arbitrage opportunities.

Turnbull [1987] dismisses the arbitrage argument; he states that in the long run the process of exploiting such opportunities eliminates them. Turnbull concluded that swaps shift the risk between the parties. In the absence of external factors, all parties do not gain an economic advantage.

Flannery and James [1984] observed an effect of nominal interest rate changes upon stock prices of financial institutions. Their findings add weight to the need for interest rate risk and gap management. See Chapter Three for more complete details of these studies.

Risks

The most significant risks to a bank from swaps arise from its intermediary role. The intermediary has two separate contracts with the end-users that are offsetting except for the fee earned as intermediary. Neither end-user has an obligation to the other.

The bank's role as intermediary exposes it to credit risk. Credit risk is risk of default by one of the end-users and is the risk which most concerns bankers and regulators. The potential loss to a bank acting as a principal in a swap is the cost of replacing a defaulting counterparty's interest rate stream (each issuer retains its obligation for its own principal). Banks may protect themselves from defaulting counterparties by requesting sufficient collateral. The amount of protection that collateralization provides is uncertain, however, because the legal status of collateral posted against swaps has not been tested in court [Whittaker 1987]. Banks' liabilities for obligations of defaulting parties varies among swap agreements. No uniform measure of risks exists.

In addition to credit risk, banks "warehousing" swaps are subject to price risk. The "warehoused" swaps are unmatched. The bank has an open position and is vulnerable to any adverse change in swap prices. The most common reason for a change in swap prices is a change in interest rates [Whittaker 1987]. For example, if a bank has an open swap for which it pays a variable interest rate in exchange for a fixed interest rate, an increase in market interest rates would lead to an increase in the payments the bank makes but no change in the payments it receives. Banks can limit their price risk in an open swap by hedging. The most common hedging device is the purchase or sale of Treasury securities whose price changes by the same amount as the price of the swap, but in the opposite direction.

Accounting and Disclosure

Stewart [1989] cites interest rate swaps as one of the financial instruments for which there is a total absence of accounting guidance. Accounting procedures for interest rate swaps had not been established by the FASB during the period of study. Prior to SFAS No. 105 both end-users and intermediaries adopted accounting policies based on various authoritative guidance for analogous transactions.

The Emerging Issues Task Force [EITF] dealt with several swap issues. Issue number 84-7 [FASB 1989] discussed the appropriate accounting for termination of interest rate swaps. The consensus reached was to treat gain or loss upon termination of an interest rate swap in the same way as termination of a hedge. SFAS No. 80 [FASB 1984] states that gain or loss on a futures contract, to the extent it has been an effective hedge, must be deferred and recognized when the offsetting gain or loss is recognized on the hedged transaction.

EITF Issue No. 84-36 [FASB 1989] addressed three questions. The first question was whether the swap agreement should be treated as an investment, and if so, whether the hedge criteria of SFAS No. 80 should apply. The second question asked whether accounting should differ if the participant did not hold the underlying asset and liability. Finally, the Task Force discussed again accounting for termination of an interest rate swap. The Task Force reiterated its position on termination of swaps. If there is an underlying debt obligation on the company's balance sheet, then the company should account for the swap like a hedge of the obligation and record interest expense using the revised interest rate, with fees or any other payments amortized as yield adjustments. The Task Force noted a diversity of practice in accounting for swaps when no underlying debt is on the balance sheet of the company entering the transaction, but it made no definitive statement on accounting for these transactions.

Existing practice is not uniform, but some practices are common. Generally, the fee paid to an intermediary is treated as a yield adjustment, deferred, and amortized over the stated period of the agreement [Wishon and Chevalier 1985]. Some banks, however, take the position that such fees are arrangement fees and should be recognized in income immediately. The EITF's opinion that proper accounting for the fees dictated deferral and amortization has not been universally applied. Despite the structural differences between swaps and futures, some of the guidance in SFAS. No. 80 is helpful in making accounting and reporting decisions for swap agreements.

Disclosure of swap arrangements is appropriate because they represent contingent liabilities and because failure to disclose could make other disclosure about the intermediary's financial position misleading. For example, a bank that has disclosed the components of its primarily fixed-rate investment portfolio might also need to disclose that swap positions have effectively changed the investments to make them rate sensitive.

Accounting for unmatched swaps should be essentially the same as accounting for similar investments. The difficulty is determining which investments are similar. The similarities of swaps and futures lead some to call for market value of unmatched swap positions [Wishon and Chevalier 1985]. Other firms account for some or all of their investments at lower of cost or market. Using lower of cost or market presents challenges for appropriate valuation. Making a judgment about whether impairment of an interest rate swap is temporary or permanent is extremely difficult when interest rates are volatile [Wishon and Chevalier 1987].

Lereah [1986] suggested that the amount of swaps outstanding, their average maturities by both fixed and floating-rate payments, and their exposure at current interest rates be computed. Some percent of notional principal should be established as a base and any excess of swap exposure over the allowed base should be revealed. This disclosure plus the repricing information mandated by the CALL report could help regulators detect whether banks are speculating with swaps.

SFAS. No. 105 [FASB 1990], which became effective for years beginning after June 15, 1990, requires disclosure of the notional principal amount. The nature and terms of swap contracts must be disclosed. Specific items which must be revealed are the market and credit risk of the swaps, cash requirements, and accounting policy requirements of APB Opinion No. 22 *Disclosure of Accounting*

Policies. These disclosures will greatly improve assessment of the risks associated with interest rate swaps. However, further disclosure may be needed. The notional value of interest rate swaps does not provide an adequate measure of risk associated with SWAPs. An analysis of the yield spreads involved and disclosure of uncovered positions would provide better information to evaluate risk.

Swap Summary

Swaps are transactions in which interest payment streams are exchanged without exchanging the underlying debt. These transactions are used to reduce borrowing, as a gap management tool, as hedges against interest rate risk, restructure a firm's debt mix, and manage basis risk.

Participants in the swap market are the end-users, intermediaries, and market makers or "warehousers". Intermediaries and market makers bear greater risks in swap transactions than end-users.

Risks associated with swaps include credit risk and price risk. Intermediaries and market makers bear both credit risk and price risk. So long as there is an intermediary in the swap transaction, end-users have no credit risk or price risk.

Appropriate accounting procedures for interest rate swaps are undefined. Accounting standards which pertain to analogous transactions are used as guides. The disclosure requirements of SFAS No. 105 apply to interest rate swaps.

LOAN SALES

Loan sales involve the sale of newly originated bank loans to a third party [James 1988]. The selling bank remains responsible for servicing the loan, enforcing any covenants, monitoring the borrower's creditworthiness, and dealing with any problems which may arise as a result of default. That is, most loan sales are structured contractually as participations so that the selling bank maintains a creditor-debtor relationship with the borrower.[2]

Banks are increasingly selling loans. In 1984 commercial banks sold approximately $148 billion of loans. By 1985 the number had increased nearly 75 percent to $258 billion [Pavel and Phillis 1986]. Loan sales for the sampled banks averaged $534,967,000 per bank in 1985. A discussion of the economics, reasons for, risks associated with, and accounting and disclosure requirements for loan sales follows.

Economics of Loan Sales

Loans may be sold with or without recourse. Payments the purchaser receives depend upon the recourse provisions of the sale [James 1987]. In a loan sale without recourse, the purchaser receives the right to a set of contracted loan payments. If a default occurs, the purchaser receives whatever cash flows the loan generates. A loan sale with recourse provides the purchaser with a general claim on the bank's assets equal to the amount of loss guaranteed by the selling bank. The characteristics of a loan sold with full recourse are identical to those of secured debt.

Commercial loans are rarely sold with recourse because bank regulations require that loans sold with recourse be treated as assets when computing capital requirements [Federal Banking Law Reporter 1990]. Also, proceeds of loans sold with recourse are subject to reserve requirements.

The avoidance of regulatory taxes has been posited as a reason for loan sales [Pavel and Phillis 1987]. A model of characteristics of banks that sell loans should determine if an association exists between loan sales and measures of regulatory capital requirements.

Pavel and Phillis [1986] offer several theories why a bank would want to sell loans. Bank management may desire diversification of the bank's loan portfolio to reduce monitoring costs and to avoid the anger of disgruntled shareholders [Diamond 1984]. A bank may want to sell loans to free up funds to buy or originate other assets. The bank may

---

[2]See Gorton and Haubrich [1987] for a discussion of the contractual aspects of loan participations and how they differ from the older form of participation which may better be described as syndication.

prefer to sell loans to fund other portions of the portfolio, rather than trying to attract more deposits or purchase funds. In addition, the bank may have a comparative advantage in booking certain types of loans and can therefore use loan sales to fund originations of similar loans.

Loan sales are also used in gap management. The value of a bank's assets and liabilities are extremely sensitive to interest rate changes. A fixed-rate loan represents an asset whose interest rate is locked in for a specified period of time. If the bank has liabilities which must be met prior to the maturity of the loan or interest-rate sensitive liabilities, then the bank may choose to sell the loan to avoid the gap.

The bank may also sell loans to avoid regulatory taxes. The regulatory taxes that a bank must pay are in the form of FDIC premiums and foregone interest resulting from holding required reserves and mandatory capital.

Pavel and Phillis's [1987] study implies that the bank's comparative advantage in originating and servicing loans, as measured by the ratio of non-interest expense to loans, impacts the decision of whether to sell loans and the amount of loans to sell. The need for diversification and size of the bank are also important. This is especially true for the 100 largest banks [Pavel and Phillis 1987]. Additional details of this study appear in Chapter Three. A fixed-rate loan represents an asset whose interest rate is locked in for a specified period of time.

Salem [1986] cites five reasons why banks sell loans. These reasons include: (1) low returns from holding loans due to uneconomic spreads on short-term bank loans to high-quality borrowers, (2) to gain an entree into investment banking, (3) to help the inflow of cash in times of tight money, (4) to make a profit on the loan sale, and (5) to continue to originate and stay in touch with customers.

Risks

Risk associated with loan selling involves some recourse to the original lender, whether or not intended. In some instances loan sales have been put back to the original lender because of a flaw in the agreement or because of alleged misrepresentation by the lender. If the contract is not drawn appropriately, banks may find that recourse does exist and a sale has not occurred. Banks do buy loans back, although there are no data on the extent or price of such repurchases [Gorton and Pennacchi 1989]. For an empirical analysis of the existence of implicit guarantees provided by the selling bank see a discussion of Gorton and Pennacchi's work in Chapter Three.

Another risk of loan sales is a function of management's judgment. Loan sales generally are generated to raise ready cash. Since only the better quality loans can be readily sold, the bank could end up with only poor quality loans on its own balance sheet. This would require greater loan-loss reserves and decreased profits. Poor management of loan sales could defeat the purpose of the sales.

Accounting and Disclosure

The basic accounting question in loan sales is "Is it really a sale?" Necessary conditions for a sale under SFAS No. 77 [FASB 1983] are that the seller give up control of future benefit, obligations of the transferor can be estimated, and repurchase is required via a recourse agreement only. Accounting issues related to loan sales have been presented to the Emerging Issues Task Force (EITF). Issue No. 84-21 [FASB 1989] addressed the question of how to account for gain or loss in sales of loans with partial participation. Specifically, the issue was whether the retained present value of the estimated future interest income stream should be recognized immediately in computing a gain or loss on the sale or recognized over the life of the underlying loan. The Task Force did not reach a consensus on this issue.

Issue No. 84-30 [FASB 1989] discusses the sale of loans to special purpose entities. In these situations a thinly capitalized special-purpose corporation is formed to purchase loans originated by a bank using funds borrowed from third parties and secured by the loans purchased. Recourse to the bank is limited (but greater than expected losses). Losses in excess of a specified amount are insured. The accounting issue is whether the consolidated financial statements of the bank should include the assets and liabilities of the special-purpose corporation in which the bank has no equity ownership. The Task Force was unable to reach a consensus.

While opinions of the EITF do not carry the authority of accounting standards, these opinions do offer guidelines for appropriate accounting for loan sales. When no consensus is reached, firms are left to choose their own accounting procedures.

The disclosure requirements of SFAS No. 105 do not apply to loans sold without recourse, the type of loan sale examined in this study, [FASB 1990]. As discussed in Chapter Three, Gorton and

Pennacchi [1989] question whether such loans really are sold without recourse. It is, in any case, an as yet unanswered empirical question.

Loan Sale Summary

Loan sales involve the sale of bank loans to a third party with the selling bank retaining certain responsibilities. The selling bank continues to service the loan, monitor the borrower's creditworthiness, and deals with any problems arising from default. In exchange, the bank retains a percentage of the payments as a fee for these services. Only loans sold without recourse constitute true sales.

There are several theories for loan sales. Among these reasons are portfolio diversification, providing cash for other investment opportunities, and gap management. Loans may also be sold to avoid regulatory taxes. Loan selling may also be a function of a comparative advantage in originating and servicing loans.

Accounting considerations center on whether or not the sale is without recourse and truly constitutes a sale. Disclosure requirements of SFAS. No. 105 do not apply.

Summary

This chapter provided a description of the structure and economics of the four financial instruments-SLCs, LOCs, interest rate swaps, and loan sales-under investigation in this research. Some of the generally accepted reasons for financial institutions entering into such transactions are presented as well as associated risks of the transactions. Finally, present accounting and/or disclosure requirements are presented briefly. Disclosure requirements of *Disclosure of Information about Financial Instruments with Off-Balance-Sheet Risk and Financial Instruments with Concentrations of Credit Risk*, [FASB 1990] issued in March, 1990 and effective for financial statements issued for fiscal years ending after June 15, 1990 are included. This information presents the issues of OBS financial instruments and provides insight into the research question, which stated in general terms is:

> Are there common characteristics of banks which predict banks' use of SLCs, LOCs, interest rate swaps, and loan sales?

This background provides additional understanding of OBS transactions using SLCs, LOCs, interest rate swaps, and loan sales.

III

Review Of Previous Research

This research searched for common characteristics of commercial banks using four financial instruments-standby letters of credit (SLCs), commercial letters of credit (LOCs), interest rate swaps (SWAPs), and loan sales (SALEs). The purpose of the research was to explore determinants of management's decision to use these instruments. This chapter provides an overview of three areas of literature pertinent to the present study.

The first group of studies provides support for the notion that off balance sheet (OBS) transactions have economic impact on the firm. These studies are the work of Houlihan and Sondhi [1984], Ro [1978], El-Gazzar, Lilien, and Pastena [1989], Rue and Tosh [1987], Comiskey, McEwen, and Mulford [1987], and Ronen and Sondhi [1989].

Studies examining various aspects of SLCs, LOCs, interest rate swaps, and loan sales provide insight into how these instruments and their accounting treatment impact the entity. Studies cited include James [1989], Gorton and Pennacchi [1989], Nance, Smith, and Smithson [1989], Goldberg and Lloyd-Davies [1985], Koppenhaver [1986], Pavel and Phillis [1987], and Rose [1989].

Finally, the positive accounting theory literature focuses upon the determinants of accounting choice. Daley and Vigeland [1983], Dhaliwal [1980], Bowen and Noreen [1981], Zmijewski and Hagerman [1981], Dhaliwal, Salamon, and Smith [1982] are cited. The underlying premise of this research is that alternative accounting principles provide managers with choices and that the choices made may be the reflection of factors other than economic considerations. The positive accounting theory does not attempt to postulate how things should be (normative), but instead attempts to explain why things are as they are (positive) [Watts and Zimmerman 1986]. The positive theory of accounting choice provides, in part, the theoretical framework for the present research.

LEASE FINANCING AND FINANCE SUBSIDIARIES

A legitimate question with regard to OBS transactions is, "Does it matter that these transactions are off the balance sheet and undisclosed or underdisclosed?" Do OBS transactions have economic significance to the firm that should be made known to readers of the firm's financial statements? Prior research examining the economic consequences of leases, lease financing, and finance subsidiaries provides support for the assumption that OBS transactions using financial instruments do affect the financial position of the firm.

This group of studies indicates that OBS leasing and finance subsidiaries do matter, i.e. have economic significance to the firm. The corollary is that OBS activity involving financial instruments matter as well. Investigations of the effect of OBS transactions upon investor decisions, stock prices, avoidance of debt covenant restrictions, financial ratios of parent companies, assessment of parent company risk, and debt capacity are presented.

Previous OBS issues were leases and lease financing and finance subsidiaries. Prior to Statement of Financial Accounting Standards No. 13 and SFAS No. 94, these OBS arrangements were of major concern to financial statement users.

Research in leases and lease financing and finance subsidiaries reflect the economic impact to the firm of OBS activity. This group of studies demonstrate several areas where OBS transactions have economic significance to the firm. Information about OBS transactions affect investor decisions and security prices. OBS instruments may be used to circumvent debt restrictions. It is difficult to appropriately assess the parent company's true financial position when finance subsidiary information is omitted. Table 1 summarizes this area of research and lists the variables included in the present research which are supported by this group of prior studies.

Table 1

Summary of Lease Financing And Finance Subsidiaries Literature

Study	Transaction Examined	Economic Significance	Method	Variable Supported
Houlihan, Sondhi	Leasing	yes	ratios	financial D/E
Ro	Leasing	yes	market study	none
El-Gazzar, Lilien, Pastena	Leasing	yes	relation to debt covenant restrictions	D/E
Rue and Tosh	finance subsidiaries	yes	effect of consolidation	D/E, ROA
Comiskey, McEwen, Mulford	finance subsidiaries	yes	effect of consolidation on market	D/E
Ronen, Sondhi	finance subsidiaries	yes	effect of consolidation on debt capacity	D/E

Houlihan and Sondhi 1984

Because leases can be structured to remain off the entity's balance sheet, firms' management may believe that certain investors entirely ignore these obligations when assessing the risk-return attributes of the firm. Sophisticated investors and analysts likely will recognize the debt characteristics of OBS leasing and attempt to add lease obligations to recorded debt. Houlihan and Sondhi posit that management believes that investors consistently underestimate the actual debt-equivalent amount of the lease obligations. They say that few, if any, managers consider that keeping leases OBS might actually reduce their debt capacity.

In looking at the effect of lease obligations upon investment decisions, Houlihan and Sondhi [1984] tested their hypothesis that investors do consider the impact of OBS obligations in making investment decisions.

Houlihan and Sondhi [1984] compared actual operating lease data of a sample of 31 companies to factor methods of estimating the amount at which the lease should be capitalized. Their findings revealed that the factor methods overestimated the debt-equivalent of lease obligations far more than they underestimated the debt equivalent. The degree of overestimation exceeded the degree of underestimation. To test whether these miscalculations affected an investor's investment decision, the debt/equity ratio was computed for each of the sampled companies. A miscalculation was considered significant if it affected a lessee's leverage ratio by 10 percent. Based upon their computations of revised debt/equity ratios, Houlihan and Sondhi [1984] concluded that firms should consider disclosing the present value of their OBS leases. Failure to disclose the present value of OBS leases actually could lead investors to overestimate the obligation to the detriment of the company. The research methodology of this study is somewhat crude. It uses solely the effect of lease capitalization upon financial ratios as a surrogate for the impact of lease capitalization upon investment decisions without establishing that financial ratios impact investment decisions. However, the underlying premise that keeping transactions off the balance sheet may be more expensive to the firm, in the long run, is an important concept which supports my assumption that a proper risk-return evaluation cannot be made without adequate information regarding the resource consumption requirements of OBS transactions.

Ro 1978

In 1978 Byung T. Ro investigated the effect upon security prices of disclosure mandated by the Securities Exchange Commission's (SEC) Accounting Series Release (ASR) No. 147. Ro's [1978] purpose was to determine if the lease disclosure requirements contained information for stockholders. Ro's hypothesis was that new information would impact security prices because of that information's impact upon investor assessments of risk/return characteristics of the firm.

Ro's [1978] alternate hypothesis was that lease commitments do not give rise to assets and liabilities of the lessee firm. Therefore, disclosure of capitalized lease data will not improve the information content of the financial statements.

Ro [1978] used a matched-pairs design of two groups of firms-a control group which had no lease reporting requirements for the test period and a treatment group which did have lease disclosure requirements. Firms in the treatment group were further separated into two subgroups: (1) firms reporting present value numbers only, and (2) firms disclosing both present value and income effect numbers.

This event study was carefully constructed with regard to controlling of industry effects and event selection, but it has one significant flaw. Ro failed to consider confounding events during the test period. Other economic events occurring during the test period could have impacted investors' assessment of companies that had significant numbers of leases.

Ro's final conclusions were: (1) the SEC required lease disclosure significantly impacted security prices for firms affected by the decision; (2) the observed price effect for firms which made only present value numbers available without disclosure of income effect numbers was not significant; (3) the information effects of lease disclosure tended to be risk-dependent; (4) capitalized lease disclosure had more adverse effect upon high-risk firms than low-risk firms. These findings support the idea that disclosure of information regarding OBS transactions has information for investors and impacts security prices.

El-Gazzar, Lilien, and Pastena 1989

More recently El-Gazzar, Lilien, and Pastena [1989] investigated the use of OBS leasing to circumvent debt covenant restrictions. The operating method of accounting for leases is a form of OBS financing because the debt is not recognized on the balance sheet, but the lessee has the obligation to make lease payments. The operating method also allows lessees with growing activities to report higher income. By contrast, capitalized leases create a liability on the balance sheet and usually affect income adversely in the early years of the lease because of high interest expense.

El-Gazzar, et al [1989] sought to provide additional insight into whether leasing affects managers' choices of alternative GAAP procedures. The underlying assumption is that GAAP is used in computing covenant constraints. El-Gazzar, et al [1989] examined a sample of private debt covenants of firms with significant amounts of OBS leasing. They explored whether the choice of the operating method of lease accounting relaxed covenant constraints concerning dividend payments, additional debt, payout decisions, and production/investment decisions. Managers' choices of alternative accounting procedures may be influenced by the stringency of financial covenant constraints.

El-Gazzar, et al. [1989] cite studies by Abdel-khalik [1971], El-Gazzar, Lilien, and Pastena [1986], and Imhoff and Thomas [1986] as evidence for the contention that managers can loosen covenant restrictions by accounting choices. Studies of contrasting opinions cited are the work of Leftwich and Holthausen [1983] and Leftwich [1983], who argued that often private debt covenants specify non-GAAP based accounting for computation of debt-covenant based financial ratios. It is an empirical question to be examined more fully.

El-Gazzar, Lilien, and Pastena [1989] examined the effect of the change to lease capitalization on key financial ratios of the sampled companies. They found a preponderance of evidence that debt covenants do place restriction on dividends, additional debt, production and investment decisions, and the payoff patterns. Accounting-based constraints are used primarily to keep managers from paying future payments of dividends or incurring additional debt. Leverage ratios including debt/equity and net tangible assets/funded debt are used to restrict a manager's ability to issue additional debt. Evidence from this study supports the idea that managerial decisions such as using OBS leasing are able to circumvent covenant based restrictions. This lends support for the present research which assumes that, at least in part, motivation for using OBS financial instruments stems from factors other than economic considerations.

Rue and Tosh 1987

Until SFAS No. 94, which requires the consolidation of all majority-owned subsidiaries, finance subsidiaries offered a means of conducting transactions off the balance sheet. Research in finance subsidiaries pointed out the effect of consolidation upon financial statements of the parent. This research addressed the question of how investors viewed the subsidiaries-as separate entities or part of the parent.

Rue and Tosh [1987] analyzed the effect of consolidation upon the debt\equity (D\E) and return on assets (ROA) ratios of a sample of firms. These ratios were computed both with and without consolidation of the finance subsidiaries.

Summary statistics indicated that for each year considered, the mean ratios with consolidation and without consolidation were significantly different from zero. Consolidation of the finance subsidiaries raised the debt\equity ratio of the parent significantly. The ROA also differed significantly for each of the three years. Rue and Tosh [1987] inferred from this that failure to consolidate enhances the appearance of the entity's financial position. The study provides evidence that finance subsidiaries are an integral part of the economic entity and that failure to include their impact in consolidated financial statements may increase the difficulty of evaluating financial position and results of operations.

SFAS No. 94 has effectively eliminated the finance subsidiary problem, but Rue and Tosh's [1987] work illustrates the need for reporting substance over form rather than form over substance.

Comiskey, McEwen, and Mulford 1987

Comiskey, McEwen, and Mulford [1987] examined the area of finance subsidiaries differently from Rue and Tosh [1987]. Their study tests the notion that investors naively assess a parent's leverage position without considering the additional debt of its unconsolidated finance subsidiary. Their competing hypothesis is that in the absence of consolidated statements users perform a pro forma consolidation to incorporate finance subsidiary debt into their overall assessment of parent risk. Comiskey, et al cite studies of Beaver, Kettler, et al [1970], Bowman [1979], and Hamada [1972] to justify their contention that financial leverage is an important determinant of systematic risk, i. e. market beta.

Comiskey, et al. [1987] regress market beta upon financial leverage ratios in separate cross-sectional regressions of two groups. The first group uses financial leverage ratios based on unconsolidated data; the second group develops leverage ratios as if a consolidation had occurred. Assuming a semi-strong efficient market, the leverage ratio that explains the greater proportion of variance in market beta should reflect the views of investors about the consolidation of finance subsidiary debt.

Comiskey, McEwen, and Mulford [1987] acknowledged a number of limitations to their study. These included: (1) data constraints which made it necessary to use book value of debt rather than market value; (2) a possible omitted variable problem (a relatively high proportion of market beta remained unexplained); (3) a selection bias (only large firms were included), and (4) insufficient data to devise an alternative test which sampled only those firms that changed their consolidation policy with respect to finance subsidiaries.

Despite these shortcomings, Comiskey et al. [1987] concluded that forced consolidation was unnecessary because investors perform their own pro forma consolidations. In fact, they believe that mandatory consolidation might make financial leverage assessment more difficult because of loss of information through aggregation. Results of the study support the hypothesis that the market includes subsidiary debt in its assessment of parent company risk. Again, this is evidence of investors concern with substance over form. Real risks are taken with OBS transactions. Managers' may use the lack of current accounting and\or disclosure requirements as a means to obscure those risks. This research lends support for the assumption of economic significance of OBS transactions to investors.

Ronen and Sondhi 1989

A recent study by Ronen and Sondhi [1989] revisits the relationship between debt capacity of firms and finance subsidiaries. The three primary issues which the study addresses are: (1) companies create subsidiaries to increase their debt capacity, (2) increased debt capacity is not all good; it also increases risk, and (3) accounting rules are not the motivator for establishing finance subsidiaries; economic factors are the motivators.

The assumptions of this research follow. (1) The incidence of high D\E ratios of consolidated firms that have a separate finance subsidiary is consistent with the hypothesis that companies create finance subsidiaries in order to increase their debt capacity. (2) The increased D\E ratio resulting from the creation of finance subsidiaries and their accompanying increase in debt capacity is evidence of the additional risks imposed upon the stockholders. Creation of a finance subsidiary changes the risk-return relationship of the company. (3) The rationale of creating finance subsidiaries is not related to accounting rules; i. e., accounting policy did not provide motivation for creation of finance subsidiaries to "hide" additional leverage. (4) Finally, if the FASB's argument that pro forma consolidations does not approximate "real" D\E ratios is true, then mandatory consolidation of finance subsidiaries appears justified.

An earlier study by Sondhi, Fried, and Ronen [1988] derived models to develop the hypothesis that the creation of financial subsidiaries is consistent with the desire to increase debt capacity.

To empirically test the models derived in their 1988 research, Ronen and Sondhi [1989] examined a diverse sample of loan agreements of publicly-issued debt. Information from *Moody's* manuals and the firm's 10-K filings provided the data. Data sources limit the study. *Moody's* does not provide data on all companies with public debt. The data presented in *Moody's* is inconsistent. Also some firms fail to disclose their loan agreements in their 10-K filings.

Ronen and Sondhi [1989] made detailed examinations of the operating agreements between parent and subsidiary. They scrutinized income maintenance agreements, holdback reserves provisions, independent credit analysis by the subsidiary, parent's responsibilities in the event of default, and termination provisions.

Ronen and Sondhi [1989] found no evidence that stockholders were committed to contribute capital to guarantee the value of assets transferred to the company. This implies either (1) that subsidiary debtholders perceive the assets supporting their claim as riskless due to the parent's reputation and financial position, or (2) that they perceive that the parent's stockholders would voluntarily contribute capital to support their claims.

Ronen and Sondhi [1989] offer analytical rationale asserting legitimate economic reasons for the existence of finance subsidiaries. They also present limited empirical data which is consistent with the analyses. This study provides an in-depth analysis of finance subsidiaries, but it fails to answer the question of whether finance subsidiaries are formed because they provide economic benefit to the parent company's shareholders or whether finance subsidiaries are an attempt to take advantage of accounting policy which obscures the true D/E ratio. Such inconclusive results indicate the need for additional research into the underlying motivation for entering into OBS transactions.

Lease Financing and Finance Subsidiaries Summary

Collectively these studies demonstrate several areas where OBS transactions do have economic significance. Information about such transactions affect investor decisions and security prices. OBS instruments may be used to circumvent debt covenant restrictions. Failure to include information about finance subsidiaries in the parent's financial statements increases the difficulty of risk assessment of the parent. A contrasting view that information is lost due to aggregation of parent and subsidiary information is presented. The question of whether finance subsidiaries provide economic benefit to shareholders of the parent or whether it is an attempt to obscure true D\E ratio remains unanswered. Economic impact of OBS transactions implies that conditions of information asymmetry between management and external users of financial statement information make realistic assessment of risk-return relationships, profitability, and liquidity extremely difficult if not impossible.

SLCs, LOCs, INTEREST RATE SWAPS, AND LOAN SALES

Studies examining the incentives to use SLCs, LOCs, SWAPs, and SALEs are presented. This prior research seeks economic rationale or other determinants for the use of these OBS instruments. Findings of these studies provide support for some of the independent variables chosen for the present research. Table 2 shows the independent variables of the present research supported in the studies cited.

Table 2

Summary of Financial Instrument Literature

Study	*Instrument*	*Independent Variable of Current Research Supported*
James	Loan Sales SLCs	LL ratio, D/E, EQCAP, EQCAP* Equity Capital/primary capital
Gorton, Pennacchi	Loan Sales	none
Nance, Smith, Smithson	forwards, futures, swaps, options	Dividend/total unrestricted earnings Liquid asset ratio
Rose	SLCs	Size, LT debt/Total assets, Eqcap*, Equity capital/primary capital LL ratio, DL, NI, NON Liquid asset ratio
Goldberg, Lloyd-Davies	SLCs	Size
Koppenhaver	SLCs	Size, Primary capital
Pavel, Phillis	Loan Sales	Size, Primary capital

*Equity capital less minimum required capital

James 1989

A study by Christopher James [1989] examined the incentives that banks have to participate in commercial loan sales and issuance of SLCs. Two common features of loan sales and SLCs are: (1) that bank services such as credit risk evaluation and loan servicing are separated from the loan funding and (2) that loan sales and SLC-backed loans have payoff characteristics similar to secured debt. A bank that sells a loan with recourse or backs a loan with a SLC underwrites the credit risk and may service the loan. The purchaser or beneficiary funds the loan. Separating credit risk and loan servicing from the funding of a loan allows a bank to earn fee income for its services, but no related asset or liability appears on its balance sheet. Such issuance of SLCs increases a banks financial leverage and increases its subsidy received from fixed-rate deposit insurance.

James [1989] sought rationale for the existence of SLC issues and loan sales in the absence of capital requirements and deposit insurance. James [1989] states that in banking, if the only motive for issuing SLCs or for selling loans were to effect a wealth transfer from FDIC-insured claimants and uninsured claimants to bank stockholders, then uninsured depositors and subordinated debt holders would restrict such transactions through covenants. James [1989] cites as support for his contention his previous study from 1987 which shows that money center and large regional banks are the most active issuers of SLCs and sellers of loans. These banks also have the largest proportion of uninsured or partially insured deposits.

Two theories predict that banks will engage in loan sales and issue SLCs in the absence of regulation and deposit insurance considerations. These theories are the collateralization hypothesis and underinvestment theory. The collateralization hypothesis states that by giving secured debt holders a high priority claim to the cash flow of a subset of the firm's assets, unsecured debt holders' positions are made weaker. The underinvestment hypothesis asserts that the ability to issue secured debt can affect a firm's investment policy and, therefore, the amount and distribution of its future cash flows. For example, the ability to issue secured debt may enable the firm to undertake new investment opportunities that it would pass up if restricted to the use of unsecured debt financing.

Focusing on the underinvestment problem James [1989] posited that SLCs and loan sales provide means for banks to avoid the underinvestment problem, which exists when firms don't accept new positive net present value investments. Cash flows generated by loan sales and fee income from issuance of SLCs provide available funds allowing the institution to avoid the underinvestment problem.

James [1989] developed a model of loan sales and SLC's that depicts the effect capital requirements and deposit insurance have on banks' incentives to engage in OBS transactions. James shows that capital requirements and fixed-rate deposit insurance increase the underinvestment problem. Consequently,the firm's incentives to sell loans or issue SLCs is increased. Capital requirements limiting bank leverage exacerbate the underinvestment problem. These requirements restrict a bank's ability to offset reductions in asset risk with increases in financial leverage. Fixed-rate deposit insurance also increases the underinvestment problem. The insurance rate paid on a part of the bank's liabilities does not adjust to reflect the marginal contribution of new investment to the risk of a bank's assets.

James [1989] developed several testable hypotheses under this theory. First, when the bank's deposits are not very risky, there will be no serious underinvestment problem. The frequency of loan sales and SLCs should increase with the risk of bank assets and with financial leverage. Second, the underinvestment problem is unlikely to be a serious problem for banks with high-risk loans. Therefore, loan sales and SLCs are more likely to be used for low-risk loans to customers with a small amount of bank-specific capital. This assumption is contradictory to the notion that the better quality customers go directly to the financial markets leaving lower-quality borrowers for commercial banks. Further research should provide insight into these opposing positions. Finally, since the underinvestment problem is worsened by binding capital requirements, banks with equity capital at or below the legal limits are expected to use SLCs and loan sales more frequently.

James's [1989] model shows that the incentives banks have to issue SLCs or sell loans are similar to the incentives nonbank firms have to issue secured debt. The model also predicts that capital requirements and deposit insurance increase the incentives to issue collateralized claims. James's model also established that banks will refuse to make some loans when constrained to deposit financing that would be made if collateralized claims could be issued. This implies that bank depositors are not necessarily in a worse position when loans are sold or SLCs issued. James found that institutional arrangements concerning loan sales and SLC issues were consistent with the predictions of his model.

The support in institutional arrangements found by James [1989] gives validity to the choice of several of the independent variables chosen for the present study. The frequency of loan sales and SLCs should be greater for banks with greater financial leverage. The debt\equity ratio provides a measure of financial leverage in the present research. James hypothesis that loan sales and SLCs are more likely to be used for low-risk loans to customers gives credence to the use of loan risk as an independent variable. The ratio of loan loss reserves to total loans outstanding provides a surrogate for loan risk. Further, since capital requirement constraints may exacerbate the underinvestment problem, the regulatory constraint variables of the present research should provide information regarding the decision to participate in loan sales and SLCs.

James's [1989] contention that banks with high net present value loans or high risk loans are not likely to have a serious underinvestment problem is supported by the Federal Reserve's Lending Practices Survey. The survey found that approximately two-thirds of the loans sold by respondents were obligations of investment-grade credits.

James concluded that his model demonstrated that loan sales and SLC issues can help a bank avoid an underinvestment problem by allowing a bank to sell claims to a portion of the payoffs on new loans that would otherwise accrue to existing depositors. James's analysis provides support for the choice of debt\equity ratio, loan loss\total loans outstanding ratio, equity capital\minimum required capital ratio, equity capital\primary capital ratio, equity capital\total assets ratio, and equity capital\total assets less required regulatory capital as independent variables in the present research.

Gorton and Pennacchi 1989

Gorton and Pennacchi [1989] attempt to answer the question, "Are loan sales really off-balance sheet?" The hypothesis of interest is that implicit guarantees may exist in loan sales. The buyer may have an option to sell the loan back to the bank in the event the underlying borrower does not perform as expected. If that is the case, then such loan sales represent contingent liabilities. Rationale for regulators increasing capital requirements may exist.

Traditionally, commercial banks have concentrated on the origination of nonmarketable claims. The essence of banking lies in the information asymmetries between borrowers and lenders. Banks perform intermediation services such as acquisition and production of information about borrowers' potential investment activities and monitoring borrowers' investment activities by enforcing loan covenants. Commercial banks perform these services for their depositors, the lenders. Depositors rely on the banks because banks are at risk for nonperformance by the borrower. Banks' incentive to perform these services lie in the disproportionate share of loss suffered by bank equity holders from loan defaults caused by nonperformance. According to Gorton and Pennacchi [1989] this intermediation role implies bank assets are nonmarketable. If market participants are willing to buy these claims on borrowers without recourse originated by banks, then these same market participants could have purchased the claims directly. The need for bank intermediation would be eliminated. In summary, the theoretical rationales for the existence of banks predict that loans will be nonmarketable securities.

Because times series data of yields on loans sold is not disaggregated at the individual borrowing firm level, a direct test of the existence of implicit guarantees in loan sales is not possible. As an indirect test of such guarantees, Gorton and Pennacchi [1989] investigate whether loan sales and commercial paper prices contain a risk premium for the default of the selling bank.

Gorton and Pennacchi's [1989] empirical method assumes that banks providing loan sales guarantees are the same or similar in terms of their default risk to banks providing backup credit lines for commercial paper. If that is the case, the variable which measures the default risk of the guarantor bank is the same for both loan sales and commercial paper. The value implied by the commercial paper equation is substituted for the variable in the loan sales equation.

Gorton and Pennacchi [1989] empirically tested the model using weekly data for the period July, 1987, to March, 1988. A regression was run omitting the firm default risk variable. Conflicting results were obtained, and Gorton and Pennacchi offer two mutually exclusive explanations. First, the relevant measure of bank risk may be effectively smaller for loans sold relative to commercial paper underwriting, even though the guarantee may be stronger. Second, the relevant measure of the borrower's risk may be effectively smaller for loans sold relative to commercial paper underwriting. Both explanations are consistent with loan sales' having lower average spread over London Interbank Offered Rate (LIBOR) than commercial paper issues.

Gorton and Pennacchi [1989] cannot differentiate between the explanations. Neither do the researchers investigate the mechanism that ensures loan buyers that any implied guarantee will be honored, especially when explicit contracts state that no guarantee exists. Nevertheless, Gorton and Pennacchi conclude that their study supports the hypothesis of implicit guarantees by commercial banks for loan sales, that the fact that banks are selling loans under nonrecourse contracts in increasing amounts seems to contradict the unique role of banks as originators and holders of nonmarketable claims on firms.

This particular study is highly speculative and fraught with methodological problems. Its most significant weakness is the generalization across instruments- from commercial paper to loan sales. The empirical tests did, however, establish a link between bank risk and loan sales. Gorton and Pennacchi measured bank risk as a function of the borrowing firm's leverage and the variance of its asset returns. The present study includes the debt\equity ratio, a measure of leverage, and return on assets as independent variables. Since a time series of financial data will be used, the variance of return on assets can be observed. The inconclusive findings of this study indicate a need for additional research into the use of loan sales. The present research will attempt to establish links between characteristics of banks selling loans and loan sales.

Nance, Smith, and Smithson 1989

Two additional studies, as yet unpublished, deal with OBS transactions. The first of these, *The Determinants of Corporate Hedging*, by Nance, Smith, and Smithson [1989], provides empirical evidence on the relationship of the use of forwards, futures, swaps, and options as hedging devices with firm characteristics. The researchers used a survey to determine if firms used financial instruments as hedging devices. Of the 170 firms in the sample, affirmative responses totaled 104. An analysis of those firms suggest that firms that hedge have significantly more investment tax credits, more of their pretax income in the progressive region of the tax schedule, larger research and development expenditures, less liquid assets, and higher dividends. Survey results also indicated that hedgers have lower interest expense, are more likely to produce a credence good, defined as goods for which the quality is important but cannot be judged prior to its consumption, issue less convertible debt and less preferred stock. However, these variables were not statistically significantly different from non-hedgers.

The authors conclude that the four instruments are not equally likely to be used for economic hedging. Survey results showed foreign exchange forward contracts are the most frequently used instrument in the sample. Futures are most frequently employed where the treasury department of the firm is run as a profit center and position taking is normal.

To test these inter-instrument differences, Nance, et al. [1989] compared the means for 48 firms which use swaps and 34 firms which use options with the means of 66 firms which do not use hedging instruments. Comparisons lead Nance, et al. to conclude (1) that hedging is a substitute for financial policies; (2) firms that use hedging instruments issue less convertible debt, (3) hedging firms issue less preferred stock, (4) hedgers have less liquid assets, and (5) hedging firms have higher dividends.

The present study does not examine OBS instruments as hedging devices. However, some of the independent variables found significant by Nance, et al [1989] have both cash flow effects and regulatory effects. The significance found for less liquid assets and higher dividends may indicate a characteristic for firms involved in SLCs, LOCs, interest rate swaps, and loan sales and support the inclusion of the liquid asset ratio and dividend payout as independent variables in the present research.

Goldberg and Lloyd-Davies 1985

Goldberg and Lloyd-Davies did both time-series and cross-sectional analyses of commercial banks issuing SLCs. The objective of this research was to assess whether banks have overextended themselves in the issuance of SLCs. Goldberg and Lloyd-Davies posited that capital markets would penalize banks for increasing their risk via the interest rate on the bank's large negotiable certificates of deposit. They found that the market did penalize banks money market liabilities when the issuing banks risky assets were increased. However, there was no evidence that the penalty was attributable to SLCs directly. Goldberg and Lloyd-Davies [1985] concluded that to date neither capital markets nor regulators view the increase in SLCs as increased risk exposure to banks.

Other findings of their study include systematic differences in small and large banks. Only banks with assets greater than $100 million adjust their capital in proportion to the changes in their SLCs outstanding. This result supports the inclusion of size as a variable in the present study. Other significant variables in time series analysis of Goldberg and Lloyd-Davies's study include capital\total debt ratio, SLCs\gross loans plus SLCs. The study employed a limited data set, but it did establish foundation for additional investigation.

Koppenhaver 1986

Koppenhaver [1986] used both tobit and logit models to investigate the relationship between fourteen explanatory variables and the decision whether or not to issue SLCs. The dependent variable was dichotomous. Koppenhaver argued that the decision to participate in the SLC market depends primarily on regulatory incentives for OBS transactions. Koppenhaver [1987] also posited that, on average, banks increase their primary capital when SLCs increase and that issuing SLCs is priced as a risk-reducing activity by well-diversified investors. Koppenhaver [1986] found that regulatory incentives other than binding capital constraints were more important in determining the supply of SLCs issued. Significant variables in this study were size, bank industry index, reserves required, diversification of loan portfolio, and concentration of the deposit market. The study showed that banks at or nearing minimum capital constraints were surprisingly less likely to be a participant in the SLC market. This is contradictory to the results of Goldberg and Davies [1985]. The effect of regulatory variables upon the OBS decision will be examined in the present study. These variables are primary capital ratio, total capital ratio, equity capital ratio, and adjusted equity capital ratio.

Pavel and Phillis 1987

Pavel and Phillis [1987] looked at data from 13,763 banks for 1983, 1984, 1985 to attempt to determine why banks sell loans. The Consolidated Asset and Liability (CALL) report provided information for the independent variables as well as the dependent variable. The dependent variable, taken from Schedule L of the CALL Report, is the memo item which specifies the amount of loans originated by the bank sold to others. The sample was divided into sellers and nonsellers. The models analyzed were specified as functions of the potential reasons for selling assets. These functions were regulatory taxes, diversification, funding\liquidity, and comparative advantage. Pavel and Phillis [1987] posited a positive association between selling loans and regulatory taxes. Logit analysis revealed the most significant variables to be size, ratio of noninterest expense to loans, and level of diversification of the bank. The regulatory tax burden also significantly impacted the decision to sell loans.

Pavel and Phillis [1987] conclude that regulatory considerations do influence the decision to sell loans. However, according to Pavel and Phillis [1987] the greatest influencer is the bank's comparative advantage in originating and servicing loans, as measured by the ratio of noninterest income to loans. The results further indicate that banks are likely to start selling loans when capital ratios are low or when charge-offs are high. This supports the hypothesis in this research that a high loan-loss ratio will lead to increased use of OBS instruments. This study posits that low capital ratios will also lead to increased use of OBS instruments.

Rose 1989

A work by Peter Rose [1989] concentrated upon bank portfolio factors influencing risk and return as possible determinants of the growth of SLCs at all U.S. banks and foreign banking affiliates in the United States over the 1984-1987 period. His review of the research literature indicated that net return and risk factors may determine change in standby credits outstanding relative to total bank portfolio size. SLCs allow banks to provide a service for their customers without booking assets which would lower the bank's capital to asset ratio. If the bank's capital ratio begins to decline or approaches the minimum regulatory ratio, then the bank will begin to substitute SLCs for loans and other earning assets. The ratio of SLCs to total bank portfolio size should rise.

Another hypothesis offers this explanation: as loan losses rise relative to total loans outstanding, SLCs relative to bank portfolio size should also rise since SLCs are not considered as risky as loans. If SLCs are regarded as a means of maximizing return, then as bank returns on equity or returns on assets decline, SLCs will increase relative to the bank's earning assets. Further expected relationships are: (1) as earnings margins decrease, SLCs will increase; (2) as noninterest income decreases, SLCs will increase; (3) as money market borrowing increases relative to deposits or as deposits fall relative to total bank liabilities, the change in SLCs relative to total assets divided by money market borrowing divided by deposits will be greater than zero and the change in the SLC to asset ratio divided by the change in the deposit to liability ratio will be less than zero, (4) a decrease in the SLC/asset ratio divided by decrease in interest returns will be less than zero and decrease in SLC/asset ratio divided by the decrease in interest costs on borrowed funds will be less than zero and banks may allocate more resources to loans and less to SLCs. However, to the extent that SLCs are a by-product of existing loan relationships with customers, the expansion of customer loan demand is accompanied by an increased customer demand for SLCs and a reverse relationship would be expected; (5) finally, a rise in deposit interest rates may lead to increased bank reliance on SLCs because rising deposit costs will reduce the net yield on deposit-finance direct loans.

The empirical data support the regulatory-effect hypothesis which states that as the capital/asset ratio and capital/asset less minimum regulatory required ratio decline activity in SLCs increases. The ordinary least squares (OLS) relationship of changes in the loan loss reserves and the volume of SLCs supports the hypothesis that risk exposure in the loan portfolio is a determinant of SLC issuance. Bank earnings and profitability generally were not significantly related to the volume of SLCs with the exception of return on assets which was negatively related to SLC volume. A generally positive association existed between increasing loan demand and the demand for SLCs. Increase in average deposit interest rates positively related to changes in SLC volume. Higher deposit costs make loans relatively less attractive compared to SLCs which normally require little or no deposit funding. A decline in the ratio of total deposits to total bank liabilities was associated with a statistically significant increase in standby credits compared to aggregate bank portfolio size. The measure which consistently achieved the highest absolute value in standardized regression coefficients was the total deposits/total liabilities ratio. The result infers that total deposits/total liabilities ratio generally has the largest numerical impact on the relative volume of SLCs accepted by banks in the sample. Net interest margins were not significant, but noninterest margin relative to earning assets was statistically significant and positively related to the volume of SLCs. Analysis of the size variable indicated that larger money-center banks are influenced in the

SLC decisions more by capital adequacy factors, switching to SLCs as capital margins decrease. Smaller commercial banks either have no significant response or increase their SLC volume as their capital ratios increase. Both largest and smallest banks involvement with SLCs reacted significantly to increases in loan-loss reserves which served as a surrogate for portfolio quality.

Although, the research by Rose [1989] is similar to the present endeavor, in that it seeks determinants of the choice to use SLCs, important differences exist. First, the present study includes LOCs, interest rate swaps, and loan sales in addition to SLCs. Second, the population of banks from which the sample is drawn differs. Rose included all United States banks and foreign banking affiliates for the period 1984-1987. Because of differences in banking expertise and resources required for entry into the OBS financial instrument market, I have limited my study to those U.S. commercial banks having $300 million or greater in assets. The study by Rose offers logical rationale for including capital to asset ratios, total deposits to total bank liabilities, noninterest margin, size of the bank, and loan loss to total loans ratios.

Summary SLCs, LOCs, SWAPs, and SALEs

These studies explored incentives for using OBS instruments. James [1989] treated loan sales and standby letters of credit as similar instruments. His work supports the underinvestment theory. The James study provides rationale for using debt/equity, loan-loss ratio, and capital requirement constraints as independent variables.

Gorton and Pennacchi [1989] attempted to determine if loan sales are really sold with an implicit guarantee. Their study established a link between bank risk and loan sales. This study seeks to determine common characteristics of banks using OBS financial instruments. Bank risk as measured by surrogate variables may be one of those characteristics.

Nance, et al. [1989] looked at financial instruments as hedging devices and examined characteristics of responding companies that indicated using the hedges. The results provide support for the inclusion of liquid asset ratio and dividend payout as independent variables.

Goldberg and Lloyd-Davies [1985] used time-series and cross-sectional analyses to examine whether banks had overextended themselves by using SLCs. They found that, as yet, neither capital markets nor regulators have penalized banks via the interest rate on the banks' large negotiable certificates of deposit.

Koppenhaver [1986] found that size, the bank industry index, required reserves, diversification of loan portfolio, and concentration of the deposit market were significant variables in bankers' decision to use SLCs. Koppenhaver concluded that factors other than binding capital constraints were important in the decision to issue SLCs.

Pavel and Phillis [1987] posited a positive association between selling loans and regulatory taxes. Based upon the results of the regression model, Pavel and Phillis [1987] concluded that regulatory considerations do influence the decision to sell loans. However, the greatest influencer of the loan sale decision was a bank's comparative advantage in originating and servicing loans.

Rose [1989] regressed several variables against a dichotomous dependent variable-either the bank issued SLCs or it did not. Several of the variables which Rose found significant are included in this study. His work supports the regulatory effect hypothesis.

POSITIVE ACCOUNTING THEORY

A large body of literature exists which explores the factors determining accounting choice. Its underlying premise is that alternative accounting principles provide managers with choices; those choices may be the reflection of factors other than economic factors. The positive theory of accounting choice includes three hypotheses. The debt/equity hypothesis posits that the larger a firm's debt/equity ratio, the more likely the firm's manager is to select accounting procedures that shift reported earnings from future periods to current periods [Watts and Zimmerman 1986]. The bonus plan hypothesis asserts that managers whose compensation, in part, is comprised of a bonus based upon accounting profits are more likely to choose accounting procedures that increase current earnings at the expense of future earnings [Watts and Zimmerman 1986]. The size hypothesis states that the larger the firm, the more likely the manager is to choose accounting procedures that defer reported earnings from current to future periods [Watts and Zimmerman, 1986]. Each of the following studies tests one or more of these hypotheses. Table 3 provides a summary of these studies.

Table 3

Summary of Positive Accounting Theory Literature

Study	*Current Independent Variables Supported*
Daley, Vigeland	D/E, Dividend/Unrestricted Retained Earnings,Size
Dhaliwal	D/E
Shevlin	Size, Earnings, MC/OC
Ayres	Size, Dividend/Unrestricted Retained Earnings, Earnings
Lilien, Pastena	Size, D/E, MC/OC
Bowen, Noreen	D/E, Size
Zmijewski, Hagerman	Size, MC/OC, Total Debt/Total Assets
Dhaliwal, Salamon, Smith	Size, MC/OC, D/E

Daley and Vigeland 1983

Daley and Vigeland [1983] examined the effect of debt covenants and political costs on the choice of accounting methods relative to management's decision to capitalize or expense research and development (R & D) costs. Daley and Vigeland [1983] used a treatment-control group design (capitalizers and expensers, respectively) to test their hypotheses.

These hypotheses (stated in the alternate form) are that firms which capitalized R & D expenditures (1) are more highly leveraged, (2) have lower interest coverage ratios, (3) have higher ratios of dividends to unrestricted retained earnings, (4) have more public debt in their capital structure, and (5) tend to be smaller firms. Daley and Vigeland [1983], using both univariate and multivariate tests, analyzed data from their selected sample of firms. The Mann-Whitney *U*-test showed a high degree of significance for each variable except the dividend/unrestricted retained earnings variable. Two methods of multivariate analyses employed were OLS regression combined with a jackknife procedure and probit analysis. The only null hypothesis that could not be rejected was the lower interest coverage ratio hypothesis. Specifically results indicated that firms capitalizing research and development costs were more highly levered, had more public debt, had a higher ratio of dividends to unrestricted retained earnings, and were smaller in size than their research and development expensing counterparts. Their findings support the inclusion of debt/equity ratio, size of the firm, and dividend payout as characteristics of firms using OBS instruments.

Dhaliwal 1980

Dhaliwal [1980] looked at the effect of a firm's capital structure on the choice of accounting methods in the oil industry. Dhaliwal compared the financial leverage of a sample of oil and gas firms which used the full cost method of accounting with similar firms which used the successful efforts method. Based upon his results, Dhaliwal concluded that a firm's capital structure affects management's choice of accounting methods. More highly leveraged firms tend to select the full cost method. This study supports the inclusion of the debt/equity ratio as a variable in the present research.

Shevlin 1987

Shevlin [1987] found support for agency model predictions in the results of his examination of the relationship of taxes and OBS financing. Shevlin [1987] examined firms that use limited partnerships as funding sources for research and development. His study used capital structure theory and agency models to derive testable hypotheses of the R & D funding choice. The sample included 103 R & D firms using limited partnerships and 103 firms that funded R & D in-house.

Shevlin performed both univariate tests and multivariate (logit regression model) tests. With respect to tax motivation, a univariate profile analysis indicated that firms using limited partnerships were significantly younger, smaller, less profitable, and had more net operating loss carryforwards than the in-house firms. Empirical results with respect to the motivation for OBS financing are mixed. Only the management compensation variable supported the OBS motivation. A management compensation variable will be used in the present study.

Ayres 1986

Ayres [1986] investigated the characteristics of firms electing early adoption of SFAS No.52 and found results consistent with an ordering effect taking place with respect to adoption of SFAS No.52. Univariate tests of the differences between firms that adopted FAS No.52 early and those that did not early adopt revealed significant differences in the earnings per share, size of the firm, and total dividend payout relative to unrestricted retained earnings. The interest coverage variable was significant for those firms with levels of leverage defined as "high" at the .01 confidence level and for those firms with levels of leverage defined as "low" at the .05 confidence level. Percentage of stock owned by officers and/or directors lacked significance. A multivariate test using logistic regression displayed an overall model significance at the .0001 confidence level. Individual coefficients significant at the .05 confidence level or less provide support for the each of the following hypotheses: (1) firms electing to adopt SFAS No.52 in 1981 have a lower percentage of stock owned by directors and officers than later adopters; (2) firms adopting SFAS No.52 are smaller than later adopters; (3) firms electing to adopt SFAS No.52 in 1981 have a smaller percentage growth in pre-adoption earnings than later adopters, (4) high-debt firms electing to adopt SFAS No.52 in 1981 had lower interest coverage ratios than later adopters, and (5) firms electing to adopt SFAS No.52 in 1981 had higher ratios of dividends to unrestricted retained earnings than later adopters.

Ayres [1986] introduced a new variable, earnings growth, which is consistent with the hypothesis that managers seek some targeted earnings goal. That variable is used in the present research. Other variables of the present research which the Ayres study supports include percentage of stock owned by directors and officers, leverage, and size.

Lilien and Pastena 1982

Lilien and Pastena [1982] examined the procedural choices of oil and gas firms in accounting for exploratory and development costs under the full cost and successful efforts methods. Their study shows that economic incentives influence the accounting choices made by oil and gas producers. Lilien and Pastena [1982] capitalized upon the opportunity to measure the magnitude of the income effect of firms' intramethod choices occurring late in 1978 when the SEC specified exact procedures that must be followed by oil and gas producers in accounting for exploratory and development costs under either the full cost or successful efforts method. The hypotheses they developed to determine factors influencing choices include: (1) size is positively correlated with the choice of successful efforts and intramethod choice which minimize income, (2) leverage is positively correlated with the selection of full costing and intramethod policies which maximize income, (3) exploratory risk is positively correlated with the choice of full cost and intramethod policies which defer expense recognition and consequently maximize income, and (4) age is positively correlated with successful efforts and intramethod policies which minimize income.

Lilien and Pastena [1982] used a probit analysis model to empirically test the hypotheses and found overall model significance at the .001 confidence level. Managerial incentive variables consisting of political risk and age were positively correlated with choices which minimize cumulative income. Leverage and exploratory aggressiveness were positively correlated with choices which maximized cumulative income. When firms were grouped according to intermethod choice in isolation, directionality of all economic variables agreed to the direction of the hypothesis; but some of the economic variables were not significant at the .05 level. When intramethod choices were used to group firms, all economic variables were significant at the .02 level or better. Dual choice groupings provided a basis for constructing more powerful tests of managements' economic incentives. Three methods of analysis, probit, regression, and discriminant analysis were used. Results were consistent across all three methods of analysis.

Bowen and Noreen 1981

Bowen and Noreen [1981] examined the question, "why do managers voluntarily choose to capitalize interest costs related to expenditures on assets not yet in service." They hypothesized that managers' choice may be influenced by the existence of management compensation agreements tied to reported earnings, debt covenant constraints, and the political cost for some firms of reporting higher earnings. Using a sample from a list of 257 companies that had been identified as interest capitalizers, Bowen and Noreen [1981] performed univariate tests of the significant differences of means of firms that capitalize interest and those that did not capitalize interest. Bowen and Noreen [1981] also ran multivariate tests, specifically probit analysis. All results suggest (1) that firms with explicit management compensation agreements are no more likely to capitalize interest than those without such agreements, (2) that interest capitalizers had financial ratios consistent with being closer to violating debt covenants, (3) that the largest firms in the oil industry avoided use of interest capitalization which would have typically enhanced its income and assets, and (4) that outside the oil industry, larger firms were more likely to capitalize interest. This research supports the present use of debt/equity ratio and size as independent variable in the present study.

Zmijewski and Hagerman 1981

Zmijewski and Hagerman [1981] used an income strategy approach to further develop and test a positive theory of accounting choices. Zmijewski and Hagerman [1981] also tested whether or not this theory is generally applicable to all firms. A formal model of the income strategy of firms was developed using management compensation plans, the firm concentration ratio, systematic risk of the firm, size of the firm (a proxy for political costs), capital intensity, and debt-to-asset ratio as functions of the income strategy. Zmijewski and Hagerman [1981] estimated coefficients of the model using a polychotomous probit analysis. The firm's income strategy was the dependent variable of the model. The size, concentration ratio, existence of management profit-sharing plans, and total debt to total assets ratio proved to be significant variables. Beta and capital intensity were not statistically significant. Further testing and subsamples led Zmijewski and Hagerman [1981] to conclude that individual accounting policy choice decisions are part of an overall firm strategy, but that the model is not universally applicable to all firms. Two of the significant variables of this research, size and percentage of stock owned by officers and directors, are used in the present study.

Dhaliwal, Salamon, and Smith 1982

Dhaliwal, Salamon, and Smith [1982] isolate the effect of owner versus management control on the choice of accounting methods by sampling 150 non-regulated firms randomly selected from *Senate Staff Report, Factors Affecting the Stock Market* (1955). Using data from firms' 10-K reports and proxy statements, Dhaliwal, et al [1982] categorized firms into three groups (1) firms using accelerated depreciation for financial statement and tax return , (2) firms using accelerated depreciation for tax returns and straight line depreciation for financial statement reporting, and (3) firms using straight line depreciation for both tax returns and financial statement reporting. Analysis of the differences between firms in the sample for the years 1959 and 1962 produced similar results. Only the results of 1962 are reported. Univariate tests of no difference in size of management-controlled and owner-controlled firms revealed a significant difference. Similar tests of the debt/equity ratio revealed no significant difference. Dhaliwal, et al. used probit analysis to test the significance of a model comprised of the depreciation method as a dependent variable and size, debt/equity ratio and type of firm control as independent variables. Probit results included overall model significance at the .01 confidence level, a positive significance at the .01 level for the debt/equity ratio variable coefficient, negative significance at the .15 level for the coefficient of size, and a positive significance at the .03 level of confidence for the firm control variable. These results lead to the conclusions that management-controlled firms are more likely than owner-controlled firms to select straight line depreciation methods for financial statements; and, further, that Watts and Zimmerman's argument for positive theory is supported by this evidence as opposed to Fama's [1980] argument for the efficiency of the market for managerial talent.

Summary of Positive Accounting Theory Literature

This collection of studies examines one or more of the hypotheses of Watts and Zimmerman [1986]. The debt/equity hypothesis posits that the larger a firm's debt/equity ratio, the greater the likelihood that firm manager's will select accounting procedures that shift reported earnings from future periods to current periods. The bonus plan hypothesis asserts that managers whose compensation includes a bonus scheme based upon accounting earnings are likely to choose accounting procedures increasing earnings at the expense of future earnings. The size hypothesis states that the larger the firm, the more likely the manager will choose accounting procedures that defer reported earnings from current to future periods.

Daley and Vigeland [1983] examined the effect of debt covenants and political costs on the choice of accounting methods relative to the decision to expense or capitalize research and development costs. Their findings were consistent with the debt/equity and size hypotheses.

Dhaliwal [1980] looked at the effect of a firm's capital structure on the choice of full cost or successful efforts accounting methods for oil and gas producing companies. Dhaliwal concluded that capital structure does affect accounting choice. More highly leveraged companies tend to select the full cost method.

Shevlin [1987] found support for the bonus plan hypothesis in his examination of firms using OBS financing as sources of research and development funding. Other findings were that firms using limited partnerships to fund research and development were younger, smaller, less profitable, and had more net operating loss carryforwards.

Ayres [1986] investigated the characteristics of firms electing early adoption of SFAS No. 52. Her work supports the notion of an ordering effect taking place with respect to adoption of SFAS No. 52. Significant variables were interest coverage, earnings per share, earnings growth, and size.

Lilien and Pastena [1982] looked at procedural choices of oil and gas firms in accounting for exploration and development costs under the full cost and successful efforts method. Significant variables were political risk and age, leverage, and exploratory aggressiveness.

Bowen and Noreen [1981] examined managers' motivation to capitalize interest costs related to assets not yet in service. They posited that managers' choices may be influenced by the presence of accounting-based bonus plans, debt covenant constraints, and political costs. Their work supported debt covenant constraints and political costs as determinants of accounting choice.

Zmijewski and Hagerman [1981] used an income strategy approach to further develop and test the positive theory of accounting choices. Zmijewski and Hagerman [1981] concluded that individual accounting policy choice decisions are part of an overall firm strategy, but that the model is not universally applicable to all firms.

Dhaliwal, Salamon, and Smith [1982] isolated the effect of owner versus manager control on the choice of accounting methods. Results of their research lead to the conclusion that management-controlled firms are more likely than owner-controlled firms to select straight-line depreciation methods for financial statements.

RELEVANCE TO THE PRESENT RESEARCH

The present study incorporates economic variables, regulatory variables, and agency issue variables in the model. Prior research provides support for inclusion of a number of the independent variables of this study. Further, prior research suggests hypotheses for the relationship of the independent variables to the volume of transactions in SLCs, LOCs, interest rate swaps, and loan sales. One of the purposes of this study is to extend the positive theory of accounting choice to the OBS area by looking for indicators that factors other than economic factors influence not only accounting choice in terms of how a transaction may be reported but also how a transaction may be structured. Transactions may be structured to be kept off the balance sheet because of the debt-equity hypothesis, size hypothesis, and/or bonus plan hypothesis.

IV

THEORETICAL FRAMEWORK

A set of *a priori* assumptions are used to guide the researcher in the selection of variables, organization and analysis of data, to facilitate understanding the events under investigation, and to provide rationale for hypotheses. This investigation of commercial banks' involvement in SLCs, LOCs, interest rate swaps, and loan sales has certain underlying assumptions. These assumptions are: (1) the market conditions surrounding commercial banks are a necessary but not sufficient explanation of the growth of OBS financial instruments during the 1980s, (2) regulation influences the use of OBS financial instruments, (3) agency conflicts influence the use of OBS financial instruments. The basis of each of these assumptions is explained in the section that follows.

MARKET ENVIRONMENT

The first assumption of this study is that economic, environmental, and market conditions are a necessary but not sufficient explanation for the phenomenal growth of OBS financial instruments during the 1980's. A number of stressful factors impacted the banking industry during this period. These factors include decreasing quality of loans, volatile markets, and greater competition. The decreased credit quality of energy-related and real estate loans in the Southwest, farm loans in the Midwest, and less developed country (LDC) loans was an important factor. A large number of major changes occurred in banking structures through both friendly and hostile takeovers. Many banks yielded to the temptation to overextend when faced with the opportunity of new markets. Banks faced increasingly volatile markets while aggregate banking profitability continued a decade-long decline that was interrupted only in 1985. The commercial banking industry experienced a 13 percent return on assets in 1987, the lowest since the Great Depression. Banks closing in 1987 exceeded the record levels set in 1986 [Gregorash and Ford 1988]. High-quality borrowers turned to equity markets and issued bonds rather than going to banks for credit [Bryan 1987].

Lower-quality borrowers who are willing to pay front-end fees and large spreads, then, became more attractive to many financial institutions during the late 1980's. Many depository institutions have taken high-credit risks as an easy way to increase lending. Such high-risk lending is encouraged by the subsidization achieved from federally-insured deposits. Problem loans are too large (in relation to earnings and capital) at many commercial banks. The large number of troubled loans may be a result of the FDIC subsidy [Bryan 1987]. The commercial banking industry had net charge-offs in the 1980s more than twenty-five times the level of charge-offs in the 1960s. The financial industry's return on equity, at approximately 10 percent, is well below the cost of capital [Bryan 1987].

Commercial bankings' economic environment has become more volatile [Cates and Davis 1987]. President Nixon allowed floating foreign exchange to replace the Bretton Woods agreement of 1944. Widely fluctuating exchange rates followed. The financial markets adjusted exchange rates to varying national patterns of inflation to obtain purchasing power parity. Exporters and importers quickly began to hedge. Banks started trading hedging instruments actively both to serve their customers' needs and to gain additional income for themselves. Commercial banking, then, placed itself in a highly volatile marketplace where risk management was more important than it ever had been. New management strategies were necessary to meet the demands of this volatile market in which banks found themselves.

A model of characteristics of banks using OBS financial instruments should provide insight into the determinants of the OBS decision. If this model reveals that banks in more risky positions, i.e. less profits, nearer regulatory constraints, are greater participants in the OBS financial instrument market, it can be inferred that bank management has offset risk with other considerations. The model may reveal the nature of these considerations.

Interest rates reached record highs with prime rates topping 20 percent on several occasions in 1980 and 1981. Real interest rates, as well as nominal interest rates, were highly volatile during this period. Ex-ante real interest rates on 3-month U.S. Treasury securities were negative from 1973 to 1979 after which there was a dramatic rise to approximately 8 percent for the period 1980-1982. Two and five-year maturities charted similarly and Cecchetti [1986] attributed the height of real interest rates to three causes. For the period 1979 through the fall of 1982, tight money was the apparent culprit. From late 1982 through the end of 1983, an increase in the profitability of investment, due possibly to changes in tax policy was the primary cause of real interest rates of nearly 5 percent. In 1984 and 1985 changes in savings patterns, due perhaps to changes in fiscal policy, appeared to be the primary cause of high real interest rates.

The Eurocurrency market grew from $22 billion in 1967 to $250 billion in 1975 and presently exceeds $1.5 trillion [Cates and Davis 1987]. This market had developed initially in the 1960s based on the accumulation of Eurodollars, i. e. U.S. dollars on deposit outside the U.S., arising from U.S. balance of payments deficits. The Eurodollar market broadened to become the Eurocurrency market. This market expanded to become a worldwide offshore currency market which generated the expansion of U.S. banks worldwide. Worldwide integration of financial markets resulted from this expansion. United States banks were placed in direct competition with banks of other countries. Many foreign banks had a competitive edge because of differences in regulatory requirements among countries [Cates and Davis 1987]. This additional competition led banks to look for additional means of producing revenue.

The changing nature of banking itself contributed to the burgeoning growth of off balance sheet (OBS) activity. Since deregulation many services traditionally provided by banks are available from other kinds of firms. Merrill, Lynch and Charles Schwab have cash management accounts available to their customers. Several nonbank firms have come into banking activities without subjecting themselves to banking regulation by taking advantage of a loophole in the Federal Bank Holding Company Act [Moulton 1985].

For purposes of determining whether a firm is covered by the Act, a bank is defined as an institution which both accepts deposits that the depositor has the right to withdraw upon demand and engages in the business of making commercial loans [Moulton 1985]. The first nonbank bank was approved in 1980 when Gulf & Western Industries proposed to acquire Fidelity National Bank of Concord, California. Gulf & Western is not a bank holding company and could not acquire a nationally chartered bank without divesting itself of activities forbidden to bank holding companies. Gulf & Western proposed and the Comptroller approved a deal whereby Fidelity's status as a fully-chartered bank was retained but ceased all commercial loan activities.

Subsequently, the Comptroller has approved over 200 nonbank banks. This nonbank banking activity served as a catalyst in the fast-changing banking environment by further eroding the separation of commercial banking and financial services.

To summarize, the financial services industry experienced decreasing quality in loans made and volatile markets. Competition from nonbank banks and from foreign banking interests that frequently had much less stringent regulatory requirements increased. These factors led to declining profitability.

REGULATION INFLUENCES OBS TRANSACTIONS

The second assumption of this study is that regulation may influence bank managers' decision to use OBS financial instruments. The income earned from OBS activity is usually included in non-interest income on a commercial bank's income statement so that it is difficult, if not impossible, to determine the amount. However, the perception among economists and regulators is that commercial banks have taken far too much risk in OBS transactions relative to the fee income earned [Bryan 1987]. Assuming rational management decisions, there must be additional factors other then fee income influencing the decision of whether to participate in OBS transactions and the extent of a firm's involvement.

A survey [Ernst and Whinney 1986] of the 100 largest United States bank holding companies provides the following consensus of comments:

> OBS arrangements are simply an array of changing products offered by the financial services industry to fill specific financial institution and customer needs. If artificial barriers are erected that differ from those that a prudent banker would otherwise establish, new products will be developed to accomplish the same purpose.

> Well-managed banks will assess and control banking risk more effectively than any form of government regulation; poorly managed banks will not. Regulators should concentrate on evaluating bank management's methodology and ability for assessing and controlling risks. Based on this

evaluation, regulators should determine the adequacy of capital on a case by case basis.

A free market approach to assessing risk, not increased regulation, should be applied to the financial services industry.

These last two comments, which reveal a strong aversion to government regulators influencing investment decisions, indicate that regulation is a factor in the decision to engage in OBS transactions. Commercial banks face two types of regulation and both may be factors in the OBS activity decision-making process. As components of a regulated industry, commercial banks have specific requirements placed upon them by the Federal Reserve System (FED) and the Federal Deposit Insurance Corporation (FDIC). In addition, publicly held banks have the same reporting requirements imposed by the Securities Exchange Commission (SEC) as any other publicly-held corporation. Accounting standards provide another form of regulation since banks are required to adhere to generally accepted accounting principles. The association between OBS activities and regulatory constraints should provide some explanation for growth in OBS products and activities.

AGENCY CONFLICTS

A third assumption is that agency issues, i.e., conflicts of interests between shareholders and managers and shareholders and debtors may provide some explanation for OBS activity. Managers are frequently compensated based upon current accounting profits. Since managers' best interests are served by increasing those profits, they may do so by participating in OBS activity which produces current fee income but carries disproportionate risks to the fees and income earned.

Summary of Assumptions
The second and third assumptions augment the first assumption-that market conditions and the economic environment are necessary but not sufficient explanations for the burgeoning OBS financial instrument

market-by offering additional reasons for the widespread use of OBS financial instruments.

The general premise of this research is that profitability considerations alone do not account for the increased volume of OBS transactions. The hypothesis of the study is that profitability measures, regulatory requirements, agency issues, and liquidity issues all contribute to management's decision to use OBS financial instruments.

These *a priori* assumptions are closely akin to the underlying concepts of Watts and Zimmerman's [1986] positive theory of accounting choice. A review of that theory should provide insight into the assumptions made, selection of variables, organization of data, and general approach of the current study.

POSITIVE ACCOUNTING THEORY

The positive theory of accounting choice may be extended to OBS activity by redefining accounting choice. In this instance choice includes choice of the structure of the transaction. Generally, there are few prescribed accounting procedures for OBS activity. See Chapter Two for a more complete discussion of accounting and/or disclosure requirements. The structure of a transaction determines whether it can be left OBS under present accounting standards. Often management can dictate transaction structure, hence permitting OBS accounting treatment. Management may choose OBS transactions, as alternatives to conventional transactions, simply because they are off the balance sheet. In other words, accounting treatment may dictate the nature of the transaction rather than the nature of the transaction dictating the accounting treatment. This contradicts one of the most basic premises of accounting-that accounting reports economic events [Hermanson, Edwards, and Salmonson 1983]. Paton and Littleton [1985] stated that "accounting should make the most truthful and significant measurements possible of the continuous flow of business activity." OBS transactions are "business activity".

Property Rights Theory
Watts and Zimmerman's [1986] positive theory of accounting choice draws from the property rights theory of the firm, agency

theory, and from finance to explain underlying reasons for accounting choices. The property rights theory states that the firm is a nexus of contracts between various individuals, each of whom are self-interested utility maximizers [Jensen and Meckling 1976]. Specification of individual rights determines how costs and rewards will be divided among individuals in the organization. The allocation of rights is generally accomplished through contracting. The demand for contracts is evident in two scenarios. First, where there is a separation of ownership and management, contracts are necessary. There is also a demand for contracts when resources are provided by both equity holders and holders of fixed claims [Watts and Zimmerman 1986]. Individual behavior, including behavior of managers and their accounting choices, may depend upon the nature of these contracts. Behavioral implications of contracting gives rise to agency theory.

Agency Theory

Agency theory focuses upon the behavioral implications of property rights specified in contracts between owners and managers of firms. When the best interests of the shareholders, managers, and debtholders are congruent, common interest prevails and opportunities to increase firm value are always taken. When interests of the groups differ, self-interest may prevail over maximization of market value of the firm. This conflict of self-interests provides the rationale for agency theory [Jensen and Meckling 1976].

An agency relationship is one under which one or more persons (the agency) performs some service on the behalf of another person (the principal) who has delegated some decision making authority to the agent [Jensen and Meckling 1976]. Assuming both individuals are utility maximizers, then it is rational to believe that agents do not always act in the best interests of the principals. The difference in the dollar equivalent of the decrease in welfare that the principal experiences due to this divergence of interests is a cost of the agency relationship.

Agency costs are the sum of the described residual loss, the monitoring costs to the principal of the agent's actions, and of bonding expenditures made by the agent [Jensen and Meckling 1976]. According to Jensen and Meckling's [1976] analysis, it makes no difference who actually makes the monitoring expenditures. The shareholders fully bear the costs as a wealth reduction in all cases. If the owner-manager expends funds to guarantee to the outside equity holders that he/she will limit activities which cost the firm, these expenditures are called bonding costs. Examples of bonding costs include audits by independent public accountants, explicit bonding against malfeasance by the manager, and contractual limitations on the manager's decision making powers. These limitations are also costs to the firm because such contracts restrict the manager's ability to take full advantage of profitable opportunities as well as limiting the ability to make harmful decisions.

In the modern, large corporation, there is, typically, a separation of ownership and management. Management is a professional service performed by individuals engaged by the shareholders to run the company. The managers' compensation provides the greater portion of value maximization for the manager. Increases in the firm's share value is the avenue to value maximization for the shareholder.

An agency conflict between a firm's management and owners may be manifested in a number of ways. If the manager is also the sole owner of a firm, he/she will make decisions that maximize his/her own utility as well as that of the firm [Jensen and Meckling 1976]. If shares are sold to others, a divergence occurs between managers' interests and those of outside shareholders. The owner-manager will bear only a portion of the cost, but will reap all the benefits of additional compensation. As the owner-manager's interest in the firm declines, his/her fractional claim declines and larger amounts of corporate resources will be spent in the form of management perquisites.

For example, managers' compensation is often made up of two elements-monetary and nonmonetary. The monetary compensation consists of salaries, bonuses, and pecuniary perquisites. The nonmonetary element includes the prestige that is attached to the position, attractiveness and comfort of surroundings, and relationships with colleagues. All the monetary portion of a manager's compensation and some of the elements of nonmonetary compensation represent a cost to the firm, which in the absence of commensurate performance, are decreases in the firm value to the shareholders. Outside stockholders will have more incentive to expend funds for monitoring the manager's actions.

Frequently, management's bonus is an important part of a manager's compensation package. According to a survey of 300 major U.S. companies compiled by Hewitt Associates [1987] and reported in the *Journal of Accountancy* [1987] 96 percent of companies have a short-term incentive or bonus plan for management or other executive-level employees. Ramifications of bonus plans are not restricted to the behavior of top level executives. The Hewitt survey [1987] shows that eligibility of management bonus plans is extended down to positions with an average salary of about $57,000. The corporate manager will possess control over some resources which he/she can allocate to satisfy his/her own wants. However, to the extent the manager must have the cooperation of others in order to carry out his/her duties and to the extent the upper-level manager cannot control the behavior of lower-level managers perfectly and without cost, lower-level managers will be able to appropriate some of the resources for their own ends. Thus, there are agency costs generated at each level of the organization [Monsen and Downs 1965]. The nature of contractual obligations and rights of the parties involved are more varied and less well specified at lower levels of management. This makes analysis of these more general organizational issues much more difficult to accomplish [Monsen and Downs 1965].

The Hewitt Survey [*Journal of Accountancy*] 1987 reports that typical bonus bases are a combination of individual performance and formula-measured financial performance such as net income, earnings per share, return on equity or return on investment. Most (82 percent) companies pay awards in cash and many (65 percent) allow management to defer all or a portion of their bonuses. A great majority of companies offer some type of long-term incentive plan. Typical long-term incentives offered are nonqualified stock options (79 percent), stock appreciation rights (55 percent), and some type of performance-based plan (50 percent). Almost all (94 percent) companies have some type of supplemental executive benefit plan. The perquisites most frequently offered to executives are physical exams, club memberships, company cars, financial counseling, first-class air travel, company plane, and spouse travel. As a proportion of total compensation, the value of perquisites represents a small (about 4 percent) amount. This survey reiterates the importance of elements of the compensation package other than the base salary of executives.

Percentage of ownership held by managers and directors is an independent variable of this research. The relationship of this variable to the OBS decision should provide insight into the owner/manager conflict's effect upon accounting decisions.

Bonus Plan Hypothesis

From manager/shareholder agency conflict, Watts and Zimmerman [1986] derived their bonus plan hypothesis. This hypothesis states that managers of firms with bonus plans are more likely to choose accounting procedures that shift reported earnings from future periods to the current period. Managers are able to do this because they have the opportunity to choose among accepted alternative accounting procedures. This hypothesis has been tested in several studies with mixed results. To provide stronger analysis of the effect of bonus plans upon decision making by managers, it is necessary to examine more details of bonus plans.

Healy [1985] examined actual bonus contracts for 94 companies to determine the actual parameters of bonus computations. Healy concluded that bonus schemes do create incentive for managers to select accounting procedures to maximize the amount of their bonus. However, accounting procedures that decrease as well as increase the bonus earnings pool for a given year may be chosen depending upon the conditions of the bonus contract. Some contracts are written such that upper and lower bounds dictate the effect of increased earnings in a given year. When this is the case, the manager will take a current decline in income in order to have a sufficient increase the following year so that the bonus is enhanced. The financial press affirms these ideas. If a firm has a loss, managers increase the loss by including all possible future losses that they can write off so that future earnings are higher.

In another context, DeAngelo [1988] found evidence of earnings manipulation by managers to paint a favorable picture of their performance to stockholders. Not only did her investigation results show that managers manipulate earnings during proxy fights in order to protect their jobs; new managers write down earnings in order to show increases in subsequent years. It seems logical to assume that if managers will manipulate earnings for their own benefit for one reason they will do it for another.

Debt-Equity Hypothesis

Watts and Zimmerman's [1986] debt/equity hypothesis states that the larger a firm's debt/equity ratio, the more likely the firm's manager will select accounting procedures that shift reported earnings from future periods to the current period. The basis for their hypothesis rests on the assumption that the closer a firm is to violation of accounting earnings-based covenant constraints the more likely the manager is to increase current earnings.

The association between the debt/equity hypothesis and debt covenants is derived from the trade-off of two costs-the cost of foregone wealth transfers from debt and the expected cost of negative net present value projects that must be taken if inventory of payable funds are at zero and no dividends can be paid [Watts and Zimmerman, 1986]. A common covenant constraint is that companies maintain an inventory of payable funds.

Dividend covenants usually establish a limit on distributions to stockholders by establishing an inventory of funds available for dividend payments [Smith and Warner 1979]. This inventory of funds is not a constant amount but a variable amount which changes as a function of certain variables whose values can be influenced by stockholders. Watts and Zimmerman [1986] cite the work of Kalay [1982] to define the inventory of payable funds. The fund is a positive function of the firm's accumulated earnings, a positive function of the extent to which the firm has sold new equity claims, and a negative function of dividends paid since the issuance of bonds.

The higher the debt/equity ratio, the lower a firm's inventory of payable funds because of foregone wealth transfers. Thus firms with higher debt/equity ratios are closer to their inventory of payable funds constraint and more likely to adopt procedures that shift reported earnings from future periods to the current period [Watts and Zimmerman 1986].

Two of the sources of this stockholder/bondholder conflict investigated by Smith and Warner [1979] directly correlate to OBS activities. The first of these is asset substitution. If after a firm sells bonds for the stated purpose of engaging in low variance projects and the bonds are sold at prices commensurate with that low risk, higher risks projects are substituted the value of the equity rises and the value of the bondholders' claims are reduced. The value of the firm does not change merely because there is a switch from low-risk assets to high-risk assets. Stockholders have incentives to purchase projects with negative net present values if the increase in the firm's variance rate from accepting these projects is sufficiently large. Even though the projects reduce the total value of the firm, the equity's value rises. Also the value of the common stock at the time the bonds are issued will be higher to reflect possible transfers which shareholders will be able to effect. This does not mean that there is always a positive price for which bonds can be sold. If the probability of a complete wealth transfer to stockholders prior to required payments to bondholders is 1, then the bonds will sell for zero. This may provide rationale for a bank to substitute an OBS project for conventional projects. The overall risk of OBS instruments may be greater, but the likelihood of immediate loss is lower. Conventional investment opportunities require direct funding whereas OBS instruments do not require direct funding. Such is the case with SLCs, LOCs, interest rate swaps, and loan sales. The expected relationship between debt/equity ratio and activity in SLCs, LOCs, swaps, and loan sales is the higher the debt/equity ratio, the higher the activity in the OBS instruments will be. This is consistent with the debt/equity hypothesis which posits that the higher the debt/equity ratio, the greater the likelihood managers will shift future income to current periods [Watts and Zimmerman 1986]. The use of OBS instruments produces current income. The present research is designed to provide insight into the relationship of debt to equity and the decision to use OBS financial instruments.

Another source of conflict between stockholders and debtholders is the underinvestment problem. Smith and Warner [1979] cite Myers's 1977 work which suggests that a significant portion of a firm's value is made up of intangible assets in the form of future investment opportunities,i.e., investors' expectations of the firm are a determinant of firm value. The presence of long-term debt can provide incentives for rejection of projects with a positive net present value if the benefits from accepting the project accrues to the bondholders. Smith and Myers and Kalay [1979] argue that by placing a maximum on distributions, the dividend covenant effectively placed a minimum on investment expenditures by owners of the firm. This reduces the underinvestment problem since so long as the firm has to invest, profitable projects are less likely to be turned down. Because OBS instruments provide cash flow without use of firm assets such instruments imply a positive present value. The presence of high debt/equity ratios is expected to produce greater use of OBS instruments.

Size Hypothesis

Watts and Zimmerman [1986] generated a third hypothesis, the size hypothesis, with regard to accounting choice. The size hypothesis espouses the larger the firm, the more likely the manager is to choose accounting procedures that defer reported earnings from current to future periods. This hypothesis is based on the assumption that large firms are more politically sensitive than smaller firms.

There are several ways that the political process can create incentives for accounting choice. An underlying assumption of these incentives is that transaction costs in the political process are substantially larger than in the market process [Watts and Zimmerman 1986]. Hence, individual voters have less incentive to acquire information. The political process's effect upon accounting procedures is examined in this context-if accounting numbers are used in the political process to advocate government regulation or administer existing regulation, what incentives are created for managers when choosing accounting procedures.

Economists have argued that the incentives to produce information and the cost of that information produce a bias in the regulations issued by bureaucrats. Officials are more likely to be blamed for a crisis that creates observable effects than they are to be given credit when a benefit is apparent [Peltzman 1976]. Failures of larger corporations are potential political crises that direct attention to the regulatory agencies. This leads to censure by Congress upon the agency as has been seen recently in the savings and loan industry's debacle. If a commercial bank failure reveals in retrospect that assets were overvalued, then the regulatory agencies are likely to be blamed. Conversely, the success of a commercial bank is unlikely to be attributed to regulatory officials. This bias provides incentive to regulatory officials to eliminate potential sources of overstatement and not eliminate potential sources of understatement. This asymmetric loss function results from the disparity of information costs. It is less costly to document government actions or inactions that result in realized accounting losses than those that do not result in realized losses. Evidence of this is seen in the high profits reported by oil companies in the 1970's and the accompanying actions taken by Congress to curtail these so-called "obscene" and "pornographic" profits [Watts and Zimmerman 1986].

The use of reported profits by politicians and regulators is hypothesized to give corporate managers incentive to adopt accounting procedures that produce lower reported earnings, which subsequently will reduce the likelihood of adverse government actions [Watts and Zimmerman 1986].

The size hypothesis predicts that more politically sensitive banks will choose accounting methods that create amounts in compliance with regulations [Watts and Zimmerman, 1986]. In the case of commercial banks, this prediction may be alleviated by the impact of a large bank's failure upon the national economy. Regulators have exhibited a reluctance to allow banks to fail as evidenced by the Continental bailout [Koch 1988].

It is also likely that the political process creates incentives to reduce the variance of reported earnings changes [Watts and Zimmerman 1986]. Political and regulatory sanctions are less likely to be imposed when earnings are steady than when there are larger profits in a single period, giving no recognition to lower profits in previous periods. Use of earnings numbers in this fashion provides managers incentive to reduce the variance of reported earnings. Large positive increases in earnings attract attention since they are used to support a crisis of big business or charges of monopolization. The large percentage increases can come from an unusually good current quarter or an unusually bad previous quarter.

Accounting researchers have assumed that large firms are more politically sensitive than small firms. This disparity of sensitivity to political actions provide managers with incentives in their choice of accounting procedures. This hypothesis has been examined in several studies. Zimmerman [1983] examined the empirical relationship between corporate tax rates and firm size. Zmijewski and Hagerman [1979] found size to be a significant variable in their study investigating the relationship between firm strategy and accounting choice. Leftwich [1981] found size to be significant variable in his study of the effect of mandatory changes.

Signalling Theory

Signalling theory posits that there is information content in dividend announcements [Modigliani and Miller 1958]. It has been observed that a higher than normal dividend often results in an increase in stock prices. Modigliani and Miller [1958] argue this is because dividends are a "signal" to investors from the firm's management that future prospects are good. Managers want to avoid decreases in dividends because this signals a poor forecast. Managers have incentive then to keep dividends at a steady or improving level. A reduction in dividend payout should motivate managers to seek revenue producing products to provide cash flow for dividends. The model of characteristics of banks using OBS instruments includes dividend payout as a determinant of OBS activity. An inverse relationship should exist between OBS activity and the dividend payout ratio.

Summary

In summary, the positive theory of accounting choice draws heavily from agency theory, political processes and their underlying regulatory theory, and financial theories to form the bonus hypothesis, the debt/equity hypothesis, and the size hypothesis. These hypotheses along with financial theories such as "signalling" and theories of capital structure policy provides a framework for the search for common characteristics of commercial banks engaging in OBS transactions.

V

METHODOLOGY

The financial services industry in general, and commercial banks in particular, are more actively involved in off balance sheet (OBS) transactions than any other single industry. Yet, previous studies have not focused on commercial banks to ask the question, "What are the characteristics of firms that enter into OBS transactions?"

The purpose of this research is to examine firm characteristics as they relate to evidence of OBS transactions disclosed on Schedule L and Schedule M of the Consolidated Assets and Liabilities (CALL) Report submitted to the Federal Reserve System (Fed) and the Federal Deposit Insurance Corporation (FDIC). These characteristics may provide insight into reasons for OBS transactions and differences among banks involved in OBS transactions. The general research question to be answered is:

Can the firm's general characteristics as evidenced by its profitability measures, regulatory constraint measures, agency issues, and liquidity measures predict bank managements' decision to use OBS financial instruments.

Four regression models were formed to examine the research question. Data for the models is based on five years of financial information for approximately 300 commercial banks with total assets of $300 million or greater. The dependent variable in each of the models is the ratio of the dollar volume of the financial instrument being investigated to total earning assets of the bank. Independent variables for each model include profitability measures, regulatory constraint measures, liquidity measures, and variables suggested by the three hypotheses of positive accounting theory. The general OBS model examined is:

OBS/Total Earning Assets = ROE + ROA + NINT + NON +
EARG + DIV + PRIRAT + TCRATIO + EQCAP + EQCAP* +
CRATIO + IBRATIO + FFRATIO + UNPSEC + LL + DL +
CURRENT + QUICK + LEV
+ SIZE + DO

Each of these variables is defined on Table 4 presented later in this
chapter.

DEPENDENT VARIABLES

This study examines common characteristics of commercial banks
using four financial instruments: standby letters of credit (SLC),
commercial letters of credit (LOC), interest rate swaps (SWAP), and
loan sales (SALE). The dependent variables are defined on Table 4
presented later in this chapter. Financial instruments can be broadly
categorized into two groups-credit products and market products [Cates
and Davies 1987]. Different motivations may exist for using the two
groups of financial products. Risk assessment and current accounting
and/or disclosure requirements for the two kinds of financial products
differ. Because of these product differences, the study includes
representatives of each category of financial instrument.
Two instruments of interest, standby letters of credit and letters of
credit, can be classified as credit products. The remaining two, loan
sales and interest rate swaps, may be called market or treasury products
[Cates and Davies 1987]. A discussion of risks associated with each of
the financial instruments and accounting and/or disclosure requirements
was presented in Chapter Two.

Measurement of Dependent Variables
The amount of dollar volume outstanding of SLCs, LOCs, interest
rate swaps, and loan sales expressed as a ratio to earning assets
constitutes the dependent variables of this study. Earning assets is
chosen as the denominator of the ratio for several reasons. Earning
assets includes all assets that generate explicit interest income or lease
receipts [Koch 1988]. Generally, earning assets is computed by
subtracting nonearning assets from total assets. This establishes an

earnings base that indicates what proportion of the bank's total assets generates explicit income. Earning assets as well as financial ratios based upon earning assets are commonly reported in financial statements of commercial banks.

Total standby letters of credit issued, both to U.S. and non U.S. addresses, net of amounts conveyed to others through participations are included. Commercial letters of credit are measured by total dollar volume of LOCs reported. Notional value in dollars of interest rate swaps outstanding measures the interest rate swaps. The measure for loan sales is loans originated by the reporting bank that have been sold or participated to others.

The probability of loss for a transaction, whether on or off the balance sheet, should be evaluated by a bank's officers prior to entering the transaction. This information is generally not available on an individual client basis to outsiders. The aggregate magnitude of exposure, however, can be determined from information on the Schedule L of the CALL report. Relating this amount to total earning assets reveals the extent to which a bank is vulnerable in one particular area compared with its overall portfolio of financial products.

INDEPENDENT VARIABLES

The independent variables are those measures which are hypothesized to be determinants of bank management's decision to use OBS financial instruments and the extent to which such financial instruments are used. Commercial banks' performance may be evaluated based upon profitability, asset management, liability management, and liquidity (which is a function of the first three performance measures). Financial ratios measuring profitability and liquidity as well as regulatory and agency issues are considered in choosing variables that are likely to be determinants of the decision to enter into OBS financial instrument transactions. Surrogates for measures as suggested by Watts and Zimmerman's [1986] positive accounting theory also are used in choosing the independent variables.

Profitability Measures

Koch [1988] cites return on equity (ROE), return on assets (ROA), net interest margin, non-interest income/total assets, total asset/total equity, net income/total operating income, and operating income/total assets as common profitability measures of a commercial bank. Return on equity, return on assets, net interest margin, and non-interest income are selected as independent variables of this study because these measures are most directly affected by income earned from OBS financial instruments. In addition, earnings growth and dividend payout are included because these measures reflect the profitability of the firm and may impact share price. Each of these independent variables is discussed further below.

Return on Equity

One of the key measures of earnings performance commonly used in the banking industry is return on average common equity [Koch 1988]. This figure indicates how effectively a company is able to generate earnings on capital invested by its common shareholders. A typical range is 10 percent to 20 percent. Banks relying more heavily upon debt financing tend to have a greater return on equity [Johnson 1989] because ROE is equal to ROA leveraged up by some equity multiplier. OBS transactions which increase revenues without requiring additional capital improve the ROE.

Return on Assets

Return on assets is traditionally used when comparing a banks' performance with its peers [Koch 1988]. ROA represents the net income per dollar of assets and can be decomposed into the bank's profit margin and asset utilization. Return on assets portrays the ability of banks to efficiently and profitability employ their resources. A typical range is 0.5 percent to 1.6 percent, with larger banks at the low end of the range and community banks at the upper end of the range [Johnson 1989]. A rising ratio is generally a positive sign, but it may indicate excessive risk taking. Off balance sheet transactions represent risks which are not obvious to outsiders. As ROA declines, OBS transactions may attract bank managers because these instruments represent means of revenue enhancement without additional resources.

Net Interest Income

The primary source of earnings for commercial banks is interest. Net interest income represents interest income less interest expense and is equivalent to gross margin for other commercial entities. Net interest income, then, is a key profitability measure for commercial banks. Net interest income generally ranges from 3 percent to 10 percent [Johnson 1989]. A narrowing net interest income generally indicates pressure on profits. A low net interest income could also be the result of dependency upon short-term, high-rate, volatile liabilities.

Non-interest income

Non-interest income for commercial banks includes service charges on deposit accounts, bankcard fees, gains/losses on investment securities, and other. Fees charged for OBS financial instruments are generally included in "other". This ratio shows the contribution other income makes to bank earnings. As increased fees are generated from additional OBS projects, banks earnings are enhanced. Managers can increase net income without additional capital by entering into OBS transactions.

Earnings Growth

Earnings is a measure of performance of the firm. In her 1986 study Ayres found earnings growth to be a highly significant variable in predicting early adopters of Statement of Financial Accounting Standards No. 52. This is consistent with the notion that management has an incentive to increase earnings to meet a management strategy aimed at achieving some targeted earnings goal.

Dividend Payout

Assuming value maximization as an objective, bank management will try to maintain a high dividend payout because of its impact upon share prices. Signalling theory [Brigham and Gapenski 1984] suggests that continued paying of dividends attracts investors and affects share prices. Dividends are paid from cash but computed based upon earnings so as earnings decline, dividends generally decline. If signalling theory prevails, then volatility of dividends may adversely affect share prices. Dividends paid should be an indicator of bank management's desire to look for additional revenue producing products in order to maintain a steady stream of earnings.

Regulatory Measures

Banking regulation mandates legal capital requirements. The assessment of capital adequacy depends upon a variety of factors such as asset quality, liquidity, and stability of earnings; but capital adequacy for regulatory purposes is specifically defined. The four measures of a bank's proximity to minimum legal requirements discussed below are included as independent variables.

Primary Capital Ratio

Primary capital may be defined as shareholders' equity plus possible loan losses, minority interests in unconsolidated subsidiaries, and mandatory convertible instruments which meet certain specific requirements. To qualify as primary capital mandatory convertible securities must mature in twelve years or less. The aggregate amount of such securities included in primary capital may not exceed 20 percent of primary capital computed without the inclusion of such securities. The inclusion of equity commitment notes is limited to 10 percent of primary capital exclusive of mandatory convertible securities. [Federal Banking Law Reporter 1990]. Primary capital, then, is an important measure in its own right and as an influencer of secondary capital, which when combined with primary capital becomes total capital.

Total Capital Ratio

Total capital is primary capital plus secondary capital. Secondary capital includes subordinated notes and debentures, limited-life preferred stock and other items. Secondary capital is limited to 50 percent of primary capital [Federal Banking Law Reporter 1990]. Commercial banks are required to maintain an average total capital ratio of 5.5 percent of equity to assets.

Equity Capital/Total Assets

This ratio measures the portion of assets financed through equity funding. A low ratio of equity to assets may indicate that the firm is approaching its credit limit and/or its minimum capital requirements as specified by regulatory agencies [Koch 1988]. This limits a bank's ability to borrow to meet liquidity needs, to absorb losses, and to grow. This ratio, which ranges from 5 percent to 9 percent of total assets [Johnson 1989] represents a measure which the financial community uses in evaluating a bank's stability and solvency.

Adjusted Equity Capital/Total Assets

This ratio represents a refinement of the equity capital assets ratio [Rose 1989]. To calculate this ratio, the required regulatory minimum ratio of capital to assets is subtracted from the equity capital ratio. The resulting figure is the amount of the bank's capital in excess of regulatory minimums. A higher ratio indicates a greater ability to absorb losses than a lower ratio. The financial markets perception of a commercial bank's strength is based, in part, on its equity.

Liquidity Measures

Liquidity management is designed to assure that adequate resources are available to meet depositor or borrower demands for funds at any time. Traditional measures include both asset and liability liquidity measures [Koch 1988]. Asset liquidity refers to the ease with which assets may be converted into cash with a minimum of loss. Liability liquidity refers to the ease with which new debt can be issued at reasonable cost [Koch 1988]. Key measures are described below.

Liquid Asset Ratios

Highly liquid assets include cash and due from banks held in excess of reserve requirements, federal funds sold and reverse repurchase agreements, and short-term securities with low default risk [Koch 1988]. Low default-risk short-term securities include U.S. Treasury obligations, U.S. agency obligations, or high-grade obligations of corporations and municipalities. Ratios of cash, interest-bearing cash, federal funds sold, and unpledged short-term securities are computed by dividing the specific asset by total assets. These ratios provide measures of the bank's short-term liquidity. The financial community's perception of a bank's ability to meet its short-term obligations is critical to the bank's opportunities for business.

Loan-Loss Reserve Ratio

The loan-loss reserve ratio measures the reserve for doubtful loans that has been established to absorb losses and is computed by dividing loan loss reserves by total loans [Koch 1988]. The greater the perceived likelihood of customer default; the greater this ratio will be. The reserve serves as a valuation account to write the loans receivable account to market. In addition to management's established reserves for questionable loans, regulators may require reserves against additional loans which are perceived to be questionable.

Demand Deposits/Total Liabilities

Demand deposits include the traditional noninterest-bearing checking accounts of bank customers [Koch 1988]. Because these funds are payable to the account holder upon demand, commercial banks must maintain sufficient funds to cover expected withdrawals. A high ratio of demand deposits to total liabilities indicates a greater need for more readily available cash. Core deposits are funds that management feels are not rate sensitive and will remain on deposit regardless of the economic environment and consist of demand deposits, NOW accounts, MMDAs, and small time deposits that the bank expects to remain on deposit through various business cycle stages. One method of estimating core deposits plots total deposits over time and draws a line through the low points in the graph. The line equals the minimum trend deposit level under which actual deposits never fall. This base line drawn represents core deposits.

Volatile and rate-sensitive deposits equal the difference between total current deposits and core deposits. A measure of core deposits represents "good" liquidity for a bank. As core deposits increase, liquidity management needs decrease. Information to compute core deposits for banks is not available externally. The demand deposit measure used in computing the ratio is the amount of non-interest bearing deposits, which is expected to serve as a surrogate for volatile deposits.

Current and Quick Ratios

The current (current assets/current liabilities) and quick ratios (highly liquid current assets/ current liabilities) are traditional accounting measures for short-term liquidity. These ratios are included in the study to test the hypothesis that liquidity is a determinant of the OBS transaction decision.

Positive Accounting Theory Variables

Watts and Zimmerman [1986] posited three hypotheses in their positive theory of accounting choice. These are the size hypothesis, the debt/equity hypothesis, and the bonus hypothesis. Variables used to test these hypotheses are described below.

Size

Two prominent measures of a commercial banks size are its total assets and its deposits. Banks reporting to the FDIC are grouped into three categories based upon total assets: those with total assets of less than $100 million, those with assets of $100 million but less than $300 million, and those with assets of $300 million or greater. The database for this study is comprised of information available on FDIC tapes. It seems appropriate to choose a definition of size in agreement with the FDIC criterion.

Debt/Equity Ratio

The debt/equity ratio measures the proportion of the company financed by creditors and that proportion financed by equity holders. It is relevant to both profitability and liquidity. Creditors are interested in the amount of debt financing a company has because the greater the debt, the more profit it must earn to cover interest requirements. Stockholders are interested in the debt/equity ratio because it indicates how much after-tax profit must be earned to provide a return on equity after debt service requirements are met. Watts and Zimmerman's [1986] debt/equity hypothesis is derived from two arguments. First, the closer a firm is to a particular restrictive accounting-based covenant the greater the likelihood that the manager will select accounting procedures to improve current earnings. Second, from the shareholders' perspective an equilibrium level of payable funds inventory exists and represents a trade-off between the cost of foregone wealth transfers from debt and the expected cost of negative net present value projects which are undertaken if there is no inventory of payable funds and no dividends paid. This assumes that the internal rate of return on the projects is equal to or greater than the cost of debt.

Percentage of Stock Owned by Directors and Officers
    Agency theory predicts a conflict between managers and stockholders because of management compensation plans which include bonuses based on accounting earnings [Jensen and Meckling 1976]. To the extent that managers are also owners, this conflict is minimized. A greater percentage of stock owned by directors and officers as a group, should decrease the likelihood of conflicting interests with owners.

HYPOTHESES

The general hypothesis of this study is that:

The determinants of commercial banks' level of activity in SLCs, LOCs, interest rate swaps, and loan sales are its profitability measures, regulatory measures, agency issues, and liquidity measures.

From this general hypothesis, the following specific hypotheses were developed. The hypotheses stated in null form are:

H1: There will be a positive association between measures of a firm's profitability, earnings growth, dividend payout, return on assets, return on equity, net interest earnings, and non-interest earnings and the firm's use of SLCs, LOCs, interest rate swaps, and loan sales.

H2: There will be a positive association between a firm's proximity to regulatory minimum capital requirements measured by the total capital ratio, primary capital ratio, equity capital ratio, equity capital less minimum required capital ratio and the firm's use of SLCs, LOCs, interest rate swaps, and loan sales.

H3: There will be a negative association between a firm's size as measured by its total assets and the firm's activity in SLCs, LOCs, interest rate swaps, and loan sales.

H4: There will be a positive association between the ratio of stock owned by the firm's management and the firm's activity in SLCs, LOCs, interest rate swaps, and loan sales.

H5: There will be a negative association between the debt/equity ratio and the firm's activity in SLCs, LOCs, interest rate swaps, and loan sales.

H6: There will be a negative association between the liquidity measures of the loan-loss ratio, the demand deposits/total liabilities ratio, and the firm's activity in SLCs, LOCs, interest rate swaps, and loan sales.

H7: There will be a positive association between the liquid asset ratios of cash/total assets, interest-bearing cash/total assets, fedfunds sold/ total assets, and unpledged securities/total assets and the firm's activity in SLCs, LOCs, interest rates swaps, and loan sales.

To test the hypotheses ordinary least squares (OLS) regression procedures were performed on each model. Several outcomes are possible. The hypothesized associations may be empirically supported. There may be correlation between the independent variables and a commercial bank's use of SLCs, LOCs, interest rate swaps, but the directionality of the association may be opposite to the hypotheses. Finally, empirical results may suggest these is no association between the independent variables and the dependent variables of the study.

Independent Variable Definition
The hypotheses of this study assert that certain characteristics prevail among banks entering into OBS transactions of SLCs, LOCs,

swaps, and loan sales. These characteristics comprise the independent variables of interest for the study and are defined on Table 4.

Table 4

Variable Definition

Independent Variables
> ROE = Return on average common shareholders' equity
> ROA = Return on average assets
> NINT = Interest earnings-interest cost/total assets
> NON = Non-interest income/total assets
> EARG = Ratio of current year's income to previous years income before extraordinary items and discontinued operations to previous year's income before extraordinary items and discontinued operations.
> DIV = Total dividends/unrestricted retained earnings
> PRIRAT = Primary capital/equity
> TCRATIO = Total capital/equity
> EQCAP = Equity capital/total assets
> EQCAP* = Equity capital/total assets less required minimum capital ratio
> CRATIO = Non-interest bearing cash/total assets
> IBRATIO = Interest-bearing cash/total assets
> FFRATIO = Fedfunds sold/total assets
> UNPSEC = Unpledged securities/total assets
> LL = Loan loss reserves/total loans outstanding
> DL = Demand deposits/total liabilities
> CURRENT = Current ratio
> QUICK = Quick ratio
> DO = Percentage of stock held by directors and officers
> LEV = Debt/Equity Ratio
> SIZE = Total Assets

Dependent Variables

    SLC = Standby letters of credit outstanding/earning assets

    LOC = Letters of credit outstanding/earning assets

    SWAP = Notional value of interest rate swaps outstanding/earning assets

    SALE = Loans originated by the reporting bank that have been sold or participated to others/earning assets much was earned for each dollar invested by owners.

Expected Relationship of Independent Variables to Hypotheses

Each of the independent variables chosen is expected to have some association with the decision to use OBS financial instruments. A discussion of the expected associations of each of the selected variables follows.

Return on Equity

The return on equity ratio is a measure frequently used to compare a bank's performance with that of its peers. Return on equity is an important measure of profitability from the stockholders' standpoint because it measures how a decrease in return on equity could initiate pressure on management by owners; and, in the extreme, could cost managers their position. Bank management then will make concerted efforts to achieve an acceptable return on equity. If this performance measure starts to decline, management may seek revenue enhancing products to increase net earnings. An inverse relationship should exist between the return on equity and involvement in OBS transactions. In the Rose study [1989] ROE was significant for banks with assets in excess of $1 billion.

Return on Assets

Return on assets is a measure of profitability as related to the assets utilized in producing income. The significance of standby letters of credit, commercial and similar letters of credit, loan sales, and interest rate swaps to ROA is that these transactions produce income and/or cash flows without requiring the use of underlying assets. Revenues generated from these transactions positively affect ROA. As the return on asset ratio declines, a firm would be expected to increase its activity in OBS transactions.

Net Interest Earnings

The primary source of earnings for commercial banks is interest earned. Bank income statements show interest revenue less interest costs, including provision for loan losses, to arrive at net interest income. This figure related to earning assets measures the return on assets from interest revenues. If this earnings margin declines, bank management may attempt to offset this decline by expanding its activity in the OBS products which produce revenue without requiring additional resources. Rose [1989] did not find net interest earnings/total assets to be significant in determining the use of SLCs. However, Rose did not test net income/total earning assets,and his population was defined differently. Net interest earnings is posited to be a determinant of the OBS transaction decision because as net interest declines other sources of revenue will be sought.

Non-interest Income

Fees charged for services to clients are a part of non-interest earnings. If standby letters of credit, commercial letter of credit, loan sales, and interest rate swaps are sought to maximize non-interest fee income then there should be a positive association between these OBS financial instruments and non-interest margin. Net non-interest income/earning assets was a highly significant variable in Rose's [1989] study which investigated the determinants of the use of SLCs.

Earnings Growth

Bank management is concerned with increasing earnings from year to year for two reasons. First, earnings are an accepted measure of a firm's profitability. The theoretical model of stock price determinant is

$$P = \sum_{t=1}^{\infty} \frac{D_t}{(1+K_s)} t$$

or discounted expected future cash flows [Brearley 1984]. Dividends are paid from cash but often based upon earnings, therefore, earnings are an indirect determinant of stock price. Stock price multiplied by shares outstanding determines the firm's market value. Positive accounting theory [Watts and Zimmerman 1986] assumes managers are utility maximizers, therefore, bank managers are assumed to be value maximizers both for the firm and for themselves. Bank management, then, will want to maintain and improve profitability because of the effect earnings may have upon their compensation package. Managers also will want to maintain and improve profitability because earnings affect share prices.

Earnings increases are important "signals" to the market that the firm is profitable and continuing to grow. If the earnings decrease from that of the previous year, the market perceives "bad news" in such a signal and discounts the value of shares by expected future decreases. If however, the "bad news" is less than anticipated, the "bad news" may then be interpreted as "good news". Managers are cognizant of market expectations and will make concerted efforts to achieve those expectations. Numerous studies have been done on the "good news" "bad news" information content of earnings. (See Beaver, Clarke, and Wright [1979], Chambers and Penman [1984], Patell and Wolfson [1982].) Ayres [1986] used earnings growth as an independent variable in her study of early adopters of SFAS No. 52. Results were highly significant and consistent with the hypothesis that management strategy is aimed at achieving some targeted earnings goal. Details of this study were described in Chapter Three.

Profitability is also a measure of management's stewardship to shareholders. If management fails to achieve a reasonable rate of return on the shareholders' investment, the shareholders may reprimand the managers either through their compensation package or by terminating their employment. As described in Chapter Three Rose [1989] found net income to be a significant determinant in the use of SLCs.

Dividend Payout

A stock's dividend payout is computed by dividing total dividends by unrestricted retained earnings. It measures the amount of earnings paid to owners in relation to funds available for payout. Again assuming bank managements are value maximizers, their objective would be to maintain the dividend payout as high as possible because dividends paid are one attraction of stocks to investors and therefore impact share prices. The ability of the firm to pay dividends is dependent upon earnings and cash flow. A declining dividend payout would encourage bank management to seek additional revenue producing products. Standby letters of credit, commercial letters of credit, loan sales, and interest rate swaps offer means of enhancing revenues. Bank management would be expected to increase activity in these transactions whenever the dividend payout declines.

Primary Capital Ratio

Capital as defined by bank regulators focuses on two major functions of capital,i.e.,financing fixed assets and protecting creditors by providing a cushion for losses. It is the second function which provides rationale for including capital reserves for possible losses such as loan-loss reserves in primary capital. The minimum primary capital ratio (ratio of primary capital to total adjusted assets) is currently set at 5.5 percent. Secondary capital, which includes subordinated notes and debentures, limited-life preferred stock and other items, is limited to 50 percent of primary capital. Primary capital is an important measure in its own right and as an influencer of secondary capital, which when combined with primary capital becomes total capital. As a bank approaches the minimum requirement for primary capital, the bank's management may choose to seek revenue producing products which do not require capital outlays. The nearer the primary capital to minimum capital requirements, the greater is the expected participation in OBS transactions. Pavel and Phillis [[1987],James [1988], and Rose [1989] found a positive relationship between binding capital ratios and use of SLCs.

Total Capital Ratio

As a bank approaches the point where additional capital must be raised to meet regulatory requirements, means of generating revenue without employing underlying assets will be sought. Standby letters of credit, commercial letters of credit, loan sales, and interest rate swaps offer such means. The ratio of total capital to regulatory capital is expected to be inversely related to the degree of activity in OBS transactions. Rose [1989] found the total capital ratio to be a significant determinant of the use of SLCs.

Equity Capital/Total Assets

The argument for a relationship between equity capital/total assets ratio and OBS activity is again a regulatory argument. The lower this ratio, the greater the expected activity in OBS instruments would be. When insufficient capital exists to finance earning assets, the firm must look to the equity capital or debt markets for additional resources. Equity capital, normally, is a more expensive source of capital then long-term debt. If the proportion of equity to capital is low, the bank may be reaching its credit limit. Alternative sources of revenue not requiring the use of underlying assets will be sought. OBS financial instruments offer such sources of revenue. See the description in Chapter Three of Pavel and Phillis [1987], James [1988] and Rose [1989] for details of the significant relationship found between this variable and the issuance of SLCs.

Equity Capital/Total Assets less Minimum Capital

This ratio represents the ratio of equity capital to assets in excess of regulatory requirements. The computation consists of taking the equity capital ratio (equity capital/total assets) and subtracting the required regulatory minimum ratio of capital to assets. This ratio represents a refinement of the equity capital to total assets ratio [Rose 1989]. Rose found this variable to be a significant determinant of the use of SLCs. Since the asset base is smaller, this ratio would be larger than the normal equity capital to asset ratio. Smaller proportions of adjusted equity capital to assets should indicate a greater likelihood of increased activity in SLCs, LOCs, interest rate swaps, and loan sales.

Liquid Asset Ratios

Liquid asset ratios are the ratios of highly liquid assets to total assets. These ratios are key measures of short-term liquidity because they represent that portion of assets which can be turned into cash not only quickly but without significant loss. The liquid asset ratios measure readily available funds to cover obligations. The liquid asset ratios used in this study include: cash/total assets, interest-bearing cash/total assets, fedfunds sold/total assets, and unpledged securities to total assets. As these ratios decline, liquidity is impaired. In order to maintain an acceptable liquidity ratio, banks may sell loans. Loan sales remove a nonliquid asset from the balance sheet and create additional liquid assets. There should be a negative association between the liquid asset ratio and loan sales.

The relationship between SLCs, LOCs, and interest rate swaps is less direct, however, an indirect relationship exists. As the liquid asset ratios decline, bank management will seek ways to increase cash; fees earned ultimately become cash; SLCs, LOCs, and interest rate swaps provide avenues for earning additional fee income.

Loan Loss Reserves Ratio

The loan loss reserve ratio measures the cushion the bank has for absorbing problem loans and is computed by dividing loan loss reserves by total loans. As this figure increases, the ability to withstand customer default risk increases. Standby letters of credit and commercial letters of credit have less default risk than loans because these instruments are issued principally to a bank's most credit-worthy customers. A higher ratio of loan loss reserves to total loans outstanding is expected to correlate to greater activity in standby letters of credit, commercial letters of credit, and loan sales. Both James [1988] and Rose [1989] found this variable to have a significant relationship to SLCs. James's study also examined the use of loan sales. Prior to the present study the loan loss ratio has not been used in empirical tests of interest rate swaps.

Demand Deposits/Total Liabilities

A bank faced with a rising ratio of money market borrowing relative to deposits or a decline in the ratio of deposits relative to total liabilities may prefer OBS commitments to loans and other earning assets. Bank borrowing requirements necessitated by standbys, which are seldom presented for collection, are minimal whereas new loans may require increased non-deposit borrowing relative to deposits. This increased borrowing exposes the bank to greater interest-rate volatility. The relationship of a higher ratio of demand deposits to total liabilities would be expected to be inverse to the level of activity in standby letters of credit, commercial and similar letters of credit, interest rate swaps, and loan sales. Rose [1989] found this variable to be a significant determinant of the issuance of SLCs.

Liquidity Ratios

Two traditional accounting measures of liquidity are included in the study. The ratios are the current ratio, which is computed by dividing current assets by current liabilities, and quick ratio, which is computed by dividing highly liquid assets by current liabilities. Both measures provide an indication of short-term liquidity of a firm. It is expected that as liquidity decreases, i.e., as the current ratio and quick ratios decrease, activity in OBS instruments will increase. The revenues generated from fees will attract managers of banks with declining liquidity.

Leverage

The debt to equity ratio measures the proportion of a firm's assets funded by liabilities to the assets funded by equity capital. A high debt to equity ratio would be expected to generate activity in the OBS area because such a measure indicates the firm may be approaching the limits of the resources that can be raised at reasonable costs. Debt is a cheaper source of funding than issuing equity capital. Because many bank stocks are selling at below book value, going to the capital markets for additional equity may not be the best solution for obtaining additional resources. Using OBS transactions offers a means of augmenting revenues without utilizing capital. A high debt/equity ratio is expected to generate increased OBS activity. Studies consistent with the debt/equity hypothesis cited in Chapter Three include: Bowen and Noreen [1981], Daley and Vigeland [1983], Dhaliwal, Salamon, and Smith [1982], Ayres [1986].

Size

Positive accounting theory suggests that size is an appropriate surrogate for political costs, that is, wealth transfers imposed upon the firm because of its size [Watts and Zimmerman 1986]. Watts and Zimmerman [1986] assume that large firms are more politically sensitive than small firms; and, therefore, larger firms have different incentives in their choice of accounting procedures. For example, an unusually large increase in the earnings of a very large bank, assuming the bank is profitable, is likely to attract more attention than a large regional bank. This hypothesis suggests that larger banks will be less likely to seek revenue enhancing OBS products. Numerous studies have obtained results consistent with the size hypothesis in industries other than commercial banking. See Chapter Three for additional information on the following studies which obtained results consistent with the size hypothesis: Daley and Vigeland [1983], Hagerman and Zmijewski, [1979], Dhaliwal, Salamon, and Smith [1982].

There is strong evidence, however, that commercial banks have incentives to become very large. In the early 1980s, when restrictions against mergers and acquisitions were lifted and interstate banking opportunities were expanded, many bank holding companies quickly took advantage of their opportunity for expansion [Koch 1988]. Economies of scale, up to a point, exist. However, it is generally believed that for banks in excess of $50 to $75 million in assets, economies of scale are not a primary motivator for expansion [Koch 1988].

Other reasons for deliberately becoming a large financial institution cited are avoidance of acquisition, i.e., becoming too large a target, higher salaries and more extensive senior management executive perquisites, and perhaps, most significantly, a demonstration by federal regulators that they will not allow large banks to fail [Koch 1988]. After the bailout of Continental Illinois in 1984, the Comptroller of the Currency indicated that regulators would not allow the eleven largest banks to fail because of ripple effects in the national economy [Koch 1988]. Banks then have an incentive to continue to grow until they reach the minimum size necessary to assure government underwriting. Size is also a factor in the type of customers served by a commercial bank, i.e., its market niche, and the availability of personnel sufficiently skilled to design and manage OBS transactions. Size, then, is predicted to be a determinant of the OBS financial instrument decision; but the directionality of the relationship between size and OBS transactions is predicted to be opposite to that suggested by Watts and Zimmerman's [1986] size hypothesis. Hence, there are conflicting theories of the relationship between the size of a commercial bank and its use of OBS financial instruments. The regulatory theory is predicted to prevail resulting in a direct positive relationship between size and usage of OBS financial instruments.

Percentage of Stock Owned by Directors and Officers
    Agency theory [Jensen and Meckling 1976] predicts a potential conflict between the interests of management and the interests of

shareholders. Managers may have a conflict between value maximization for themselves and value maximization for the firm. Management compensation schemes frequently include bonuses based upon accounting earnings. This criteria for additional compensation may cause management to concentrate upon maintaining an attractive "bottom-line" to the detriment of the long run profitability and liquidity of the firm. For support of Watts and Zimmerman's [1986] bonus plan hypothesis see descriptions of studies by Ayres, [1986] Dhaliwal, Salamon, and Smith [1982] in Chapter Three.

Seeking OBS products which generate revenues and/or immediate cash flows without utilizing assets at risks disproportionate to the revenues and cash flows produced is not in the best interests of owners. To the extent that managers are also owners, this conflict is minimized. There should be a negative association between the degree of management ownership and OBS transactions.

Managers who do not own stock or who own inconsequential amounts of stock are more likely to concentrate on short term profits when part of their compensation package is a bonus based upon accounting earnings. These managers have a conflict between what is in their best interest-higher immediate profits-and what is in the best interests of the shareholders-long-term profitability and liquidity. A greater percentage of stock owned by managers and directors as a group would predict less participation in OBS revenue enhancing products such as standby letters of credit, commercial letters of credit, and interest rate swaps. If use of these products also enhances long-run profits, then there is no conflict between managers and shareholders. There may be long-run benefits from these products in that they serve a customer demand, help to retain customers, and maintain ongoing business for the bank. However, future benefits are uncertain, uncertainty represents risk, and the risk/return tradeoff might be unacceptable to present and future shareholders if that risk/return relationship were known to them.

It is not uncommon in the financial services industry for size of asset pools to be a factor in bonus computation for managers [Cates and Davis 1987]. Because the size of asset pools is a factor in bonuses, bank management may be reluctant to securitize assets even when the immediate cash flow and servicing fees would enhance the liquidity and profitability of the bank. A greater proportion of management and director-owned stock to total stock would predict less participation in loan sales.

DATA COLLECTION AND SAMPLE SELECTION

The primary database used for this study was magnetic tapes of Consolidated Asset and Liability (CALL) Reports of domestic commercial banks having assets greater than $300 million. Several reasons support this choice of population. First, the financial instruments under scrutiny require sufficient expertise of bank personnel to appropriately structure the transaction. Second, the most likely customers requiring a bank's intermediary services to participate in off balance sheet (OBS) financial instruments are large corporations. Large corporations are more likely to seek large banks to provide financial services. Third, when a bank is not functioning as an intermediary but entering into OBS financial transactions as a primary participant, the bank should have sufficient underlying resources to absorb potential losses. Because regulatory constraints require a minimum percentage of equity, greater total assets equates to greater amounts of equity when measured in dollars. This provides a greater cushion to absorb losses.

Reducing the total population of domestic commercial banks to those with assets equal to or in excess of $300 million resulted in a group of approximately 1700 observations. A random sample of banks was selected from this group. Two independent random starts were used to eliminate any bias in this listing. The initial banks chosen were followed throughout the years under examination, 1984 through 1988. The starting point chosen was, 1986, the midpoint of the years being studied. The choice of a midpoint from which to draw the sample reduces possible survivorship bias in the study. The random sampling yielded from 375 to 377 initial observations for the years being examined. If an observation did not meet the criteria of assets equal to or greater than $300 million for all years being examined, it was included only for those years in which the criterion was met. For example, if two smaller banks merged to become a bank with assets equal to or greater than $300 million in 1986, the smaller constituent banks were not included in the 1984 and 1985 samples. This research considered each institution's data independently at each given point in time.

The corporate affiliations of each bank included in the study were researched through the *Directory of Corporate Affiliations*. Additional information as to ownership and corporate affiliations was determined by examination of information available on each bank in the sample in *Moody's Bank & Finance Manual.*

One of the independent variables of this research, the percentage of stock owned by directors and officers as a group, was taken from proxy statements of the institutions included in the sample. Banks, which are not publicly held, file no proxy statement; therefore, this variable does not appear for those banks.

Other institutions are wholly-owned subsidiaries of holding companies. Information from proxy statements of the holding or "parent" company revealed the percentage of stock owned by directors and officers as a group for these institutions.

The proxy statements located in microfiche files published by *Disclosure,* for the years 1984 through 1986 provided the source for the percentage of stock owned by officers and directors as a group. Beginning in 1987, *Disclosure* published an electronic database. The targeted proxy statements, located on this database, provide the independent variable, percentage of stock owned by directors and officers as a group for the years 1987 and 1988. Each of the other independent variables as well as the dependent variables were computed from financial data included on the CALL reports of the selected commercial banks.

The parameters of the study are dictated by the availability of the FDIC tapes. Interest rate swap disclosure requirements in CALL reports became effective in 1985. For swaps, then, the period of study is 1985 through 1988; for each of the other dependent variables, it is 1984 through 1988.

EMPIRICAL MODEL AND DATA ANALYSIS

The general OBS model to be examined is:
OBS/Total Assets = ROE + ROA + NINT + NON + EARG + DIV + PRIRAT + TCRATIO + EQCAP + EQCAP* + CRATIO + IBRATIO + FFRATIO + UNPSEC + LL + DL + CURRENT + QUICK + LEV + SIZE + D0

The variables are defined in Table 4. The following specific models were used to empirically test the characteristics evidenced by the independent variables for each of the OBS instruments examined. The models which were examined are:

SLC/TOTAL ASSETS = $\beta 0$ + $\beta 1$ROE + $\beta 2$ROA + $\beta 3$NINT + $\beta 4$NON + $\beta 5$EARG + $\beta 6$DIV + $\beta 7$PRIRAT + $\beta 8$TCRATIO + $\beta 9$EQCAP + $\beta 10$EQCAP* + $\beta 11$CRATIO + $\beta 12$IBRATIO + $\beta 13$FFRATIO + $\beta 14$UNPSEC + $\beta 15$LL + $\beta 16$DL + $\beta 17$CURRENT + $\beta 18$QUICK + $\beta 19$LEV + $\beta 20$SIZE + $\beta 21$DO

LOC/TOTAL ASSETS = $\beta 0$ + $\beta 1$ROE + $\beta 2$ROA + $\beta 3$NINT + $\beta 4$NON + $\beta 5$EARG + $\beta 6$DIV + $\beta 7$PRIRAT + $\beta 8$TCRATIO + $\beta 9$EQCAP + $\beta 10$EQCAP* + $\beta 11$CRATIO + $\beta 12$IBRATIO + $\beta 13$FFRATIO + $\beta 14$UNPSEC + $\beta 15$LL + $\beta 16$DL + $\beta 17$CURRENT + $\beta 18$QUICK + $\beta 19$LEV + $\beta 20$SIZE + $\beta 21$DO

SWAP/TOTAL ASSETS = $\beta 0$ + $\beta 1$ROE + $\beta 2$ROA + $\beta 3$NINT + $\beta 4$NON + $\beta 5$EARG + $\beta 6$DIV + $\beta 7$PRIRAT + $\beta 8$TCRATIO + $\beta 9$EQCAP + $\beta 10$EQCAP* + $\beta 11$CRATIO + $\beta 12$IBRATIO + $\beta 13$FFRATIO + $\beta 14$UNPSEC + $\beta 15$LL + $\beta 16$DL + $\beta 17$CURRENT + $\beta 18$QUICK + $\beta 19$LEV + $\beta 20$SIZE + $\beta 21$DO

SALE/TOTAL ASSETS = $\beta 0$ + $\beta 1$ROE + $\beta 2$ROA + $\beta 3$NINT + $\beta 4$NON + $\beta 5$EARG + $\beta 6$DIV + $\beta 7$PRIRAT + $\beta 8$TCRATIO + $\beta 9$EQCAP + $\beta 10$EQCAP* + $\beta 11$CRATIO + $\beta 12$IBRATIO + $\beta 13$FFRATIO + $\beta 14$UNPSEC + $\beta 15$LL + $\beta 16$DL + $\beta 17$CURRENT + $\beta 18$QUICK + $\beta 19$LEV + $\beta 20$SIZE + $\beta 21$DO

Selection of Statistical Analysis Procedure

Several methods are available to simultaneously test the significance of the variables developed from the hypotheses. The purpose of the empirical tests is to form a model of common characteristics which may determine whether managers choose transactions structured to remain off the balance sheet, as opposed to choosing alternative financial products and services. In many accounting choice studies the dependent variable is dichotomous, i.e. either the firm did or did not make a certain choice. In such cases numerous researchers (appropriately) have chosen a form of binary regression to analyze their data. The majority of accounting choice studies have employed either probit or logit analysis as the statistical analysis tool of choice. (See Ayres [1986], Deakin [1989], Kelly [1985], Zmijewski and Hagerman [1981],and Bowen and Noreen [1981].) In this study, the dependent variable is expressed as a ratio of the financial instrument to total earning assets. Both the numerator and denominator of the dependent variable fraction comprising the ratio are continuous variables. Multiple regression analysis provides the appropriate statistical tool for data of this nature. Because multiple regression is the statistical analysis technique with the greatest power to reject a null hypothesis, it has been widely used throughout the accounting and finance literature. James [1988], Comiskey, McEwen, and Mulford [1987], and Lilien and Pastena [1982] used probit, multiple discriminant analysis, and ordinary least squares regression with little differences among the three techniques.

Since most of the independent variables of the study are formed from financial data, a high probability exists of multicolllinearity among the variables. The presence of high correlation among the independent variables would present misleading beta estimates and standard errors. Tests for multicollinearity were performed as part of the OLS regressions. Since, as expected, severe multicollinearity was present among some of the variables, additional tests were indicated.

Factor analysis is an appropriate analytical tool for exploratory research [Jackson 1983] such as the present study. The resulting factor scores then serve as independent variables in a multiple regression analysis. This procedure eliminates the interdependence of the independent variables.

Factor analysis provided an effective methodology for eliminating multicollinearity among the independent variables.

VI

DATA ANALYSIS AND INTERPRETATION

The general research question addressed by this study is:

Can a firm's general characteristics as measured by its profitability measures, regulatory measures, agency issues, and liquidity measures predict bank managements' decision to use OBS financial instruments.

The OBS financial instruments examined are standby letters of credit (SLC), letters of credit (LOC), interest rate swaps (SWAP), and loan sales (SALE).

Models of the common characteristics of commercial banks which used these four financial instruments were developed from a series of statistical procedures. The models are presented in Table 5. The table lists each of the dependent variables of the study-the financial instruments. Common characteristics of banks engaging in OBS transactions of each of the instruments are listed.

Table 5

Models of Common Characteristics
By Financial Instrument

SLC	LOC	SWAP	SALE
Capital	Capital	Capital	Capital
Liquid Assets	Liquid Assets	Liquid Assets	Liquid Assets
Performance			

STATISTICAL PROCEDURES

The series of statistical tests performed identified common characteristics of banks entering into off balance
sheet (OBS) transactions. Statistical tests performed included: (1) a Pearson's product moment correlation test of the independent variables; (2) ordinary least squares (OLS) regression of the independent variables against each of the dependent variables, i.e., SLC/EA, LOC/EA, SWAP/EA, and SALE/EA; (3) factor analysis of the independent variables; and (4) an OLS regression of the resulting factors against each of the four dependent variables.

Pearson Product Moment Correlation

The correlation procedure identified independent variables which were highly correlated to each other. The purpose of the test was to eliminate variables which were so highly correlated that the variables measure essentially the same data.

The correlation procedure revealed that equity capital, adjusted equity capital and total capital were highly correlated to each other (.669 to .920). Inclusion of all three variables would be redundant. Total capital ratio (Tcratio) becomes the variable of choice for two reasons. First, total capital ratio represents a valid measure of a bank's capital. Second, this ratio is calculated in accordance with specific regulatory requirements. Since the general research question addresses the issue of regulatory measures' affect upon the OBS transaction decision, total capital ratio provides the appropriate measure of capital. Primary capital (Prirat) also is included because it represents a different constraint placed upon banks by regulators. Other variables were not unusually highly correlated to each other.

Since 1984 is the base year of this study, no previous year's earnings figures were available to compute earnings growth. The absolute value of earnings was used as a proxy variable for earnings growth. However, earnings proved to be reflective of size of the firm rather then a measure of performance. The earnings figure, therefore, was eliminated as a variable.

The set of variables included in the initial analyses include: total capital ratio (Tcratio), primary capital ratio (Prirat), cash/total assets (Cratio); interest-bearing cash/total assets (Ibratio), unpledged securities/total assets (Unpsec); loan-loss reserve ratio (LL); debt/equity ratio (LEV); percentage of stock owned by officers and directors as a group (DO); current ratio (Current); quick ratio (Quick); Net interest income (Nint); non-interest income (NON); Size, Earnings growth (Earg) 1985-1988; return on assets (ROA); return on equity (ROE), and dividend payout ratio (DIV). These variables and the expected relationship of the independent variables to each of the dependent variables are more fully described in Chapter Five.

OLS Regression

The second step of the analyses regressed the full model of independent variables against each of the dependent variables. Four regressions were run for each of the five years examined-one regression for each of the dependent variables (SLC, LOC, SWAP, and SALE). In each of the years examined a number of the independent variables reflected variance inflation levels (VIF) of 1.5 or greater. A variance inflation level of 1.5 indicates serious multicollinearity and exceeds the maximum value generally accepted for statistical interpretation. This correlation among the independent variables prohibits interpretation of the individual parameter estimates and *p*-values of the independent variables. As discussed in Chapter Five, an acceptable analytical approach in these circumstances is to perform factor analysis of the independent variables and use the resulting factors in the model as independent variables.

The percentage of stock owned by directors and officers as a group (DO) failed to enter any of the regression models. This coupled with the observation that these percentages were almost all less than one percent provided support for elimination of this variable from further analysis.

Factor Analysis

The fundamental idea of factor analysis is that the members of a group of variables have certain underlying, unobservable common constructs which determine some, if not all, of their structure [Jackson 1983]. These common constructs are called factors. The simple factor analytic model assumes that correlations among a set of variables are explained by a common factor. The aim of factor analysis is to analyze the internal structure of the set of variables to identify this underlying construct.

Data reduction and summarization is the primary purpose of factor analysis. The factor analysis procedure searches for and defines the fundamental constructs underlying the original variables with a minimum loss of information. The product of factor analysis provides appropriate variables for subsequent regression procedures. Factor analysis groups variables together so that there is minimum variation of the variables within the factor and maximum variance between the factors. This maximum variation between factors eliminates the interdependence of the variables thereby eliminating multicollinearity. The independent factors provide a valid basis for interpretation of parameter estimates and *p*-values in subsequent regressions.

Factor loading scores of .5 or greater of the independent variables determine which variables are included in a factor. Names given to factors represent, to the extent possible, the common underlying construct of the variables loading into a factor. Generally, variables with higher loading scores are given more consideration in naming factors than those with lower loading scores. The factor names assigned are subjective judgments based on which variables load together to comprise a factor and the logical relationship of these variables to each other.

A varimax rotation method was used because the purpose of the factor analysis was to maximize variation between factors with a minimum number of iterations. Quartermax rotation computes the variance of the loadings across each row and down each column as the varimax criterion does [Jackson 1983]. Its effect is to increase the variability of the loadings throughout the matrix. Quartermax is preferred when the researcher suspects the presence of a general factor. However, nothing in the data suggested a general factor. This research concentrates on the variables, hence, varimax rotation provides the criterion by which the variables are analyzed.

Factor Analysis Results

The rotated factor patterns emerging from a varimax rotation for each of the years of this research, 1984-1988, are summarized and presented on Table 6. Generally, the independent variables loaded consistently into the same factors throughout the period of study. However, some inconsistences exist. Table 6 reflects each of the variables which loaded into a factor as well as each of the years that variable loaded into the given factor. The presence of an asterisk (*) indicates that the variable loaded into that particular factor for all the years studied. Performance proved to be a common characteristic of banks using SLCs. Capital and liquid assets were common characteristics of banks using SLCs, LOCs, SWAPs, and SALEs. None of the other factors were judged to be common characteristics of banks involved in OBS transactions of the four financial instruments studied.

Table 6

Composition of Factors by Year

Performance	*Capital*	*Liquid Assets*
ROA*	Tcratio*	Cratio*
ROE*	Prirat*	Ibratio*
LL 1986-1988	Size 1984-1986,1988	Unpsec 1984
		NINT 1984
SLC**	SLC,LOC,SWAP, SALE**	SLC,LOC,SWAP, SALE**

Liquidity	*Excess Funds*	*Dividend*
Current*	Ffratio 1984,1985,1988	DIV*
Quick*	Unpsec 1985	DO 1988

Cash Demands	*Leverage*	*Earnings Growth*
LL 1984	D/L 1984	Earg 1985-1988
D/L 1984-1987		LL 1985
Ffratio 1986, 1987		NINT 1985
		NON 1987
		D/L 1988

Income Components
NON 1986, 1988
NINT 1986-1988
Unpsec 1987

*This variable is included in this factor for all years.
**Dependent variable for which this is a common characteristic.

The following discussion describes the resulting factors and addresses the consistences and inconsistencies of the factor loadings.

Liquidity Measures

The independent variables current ratio (current) and quick ratio (quick) consistently loaded together into a factor. Since these variables are traditional accounting measures for liquidity, the resulting factor is named Liquidity.

Liquid Assets

Two measures of asset liquidity, cash/total assets (Cratio) and interest-bearing cash/total assets (Ibratio) load into the same factor consistently throughout the period of study. In 1984 unpledged securities (Unpsec) and Net interest income (Nint) also load into the same factor. Unpledged securities is a highly liquid asset and its correlation to the same underlying factor as the cash measures is not unexpected. Liquid assets by definition have less risk than other assets. Interest income decreases as risk decreases; therefore, as liquid assets increase, net interest income decreases. The primary source of earnings for a commercial bank in 1984 was its interest income, which made up an average of 4.31 percent of net income for this sampling of banks. By 1987, the percentage of net interest to net income had dropped to 2.89 percent. Net interest represents interest income less interest expense, a commercial bank's gross margin. Loans, the principal source of interest income, are not readily liquidated. The negative relationship of net interest to liquid assets is reasonable. This factor is called "Liquid Assets".

Capital Measures

The variables debt/equity (LEV), primary ratio (Prirat), and total capital ratio (Tcratio) group together in all years except 1984 when D/E makes up a separate factor. The close association of capital risk with leverage accounts for the inclusion of the debt/equity ratio in the capital factor. The independent variable SIZE aligns with the capital measures in 1984 and 1985. In subsequent years SIZE fragments across several factors so that it is not included in any single factor. However, the highest factor loading score for SIZE continues to be with the "Capital" factor.

Performance

The factor named "Performance" consists of return on assets (ROA) and return on equity (ROE) for each of the five years examined. The required addition to loan-loss reserve represents a significant determinant of net income and is a measure of loan performance. The inclusion of loan-loss reserve ratio (LL) in 1986, 1987, 1988, is reasonable in view of the banking environment during those years. Historically, commercial banks loan-loss reserves average less than one percent of total assets. In 1986, 1987, and 1988 the average for the sampled banks was .9 percent, 1.25 percent, and 1.26 percent, respectively. The most appropriate name for this factor appears to be "Performance" since ROA and ROE are widely accepted measures of performance.

Income Components

Net interest income (Nint) and non-interest income (Non) represent two broad categories of income. These independent variables form a separate factor in 1986 and 1988. Non-interest income fragments in 1984, and net interest income aligns with liquid assets. In 1985 both categories of income align with earnings growth and loan-loss reserve. The higher factor loading score of earnings growth suggests that the appropriate name for that factor is "earnings growth". In 1987 non-interest income aligns with earnings growth again, while net interest and unpledged securities form another factor. The factor "income components" is not significant in the model.

Earnings Growth

As previously discussed, no earnings growth variable is available for 1984. In 1985 earnings growth forms a factor including earnings growth, loan-loss reserve ratio, net interest income and non-interest income. Since loan-losses directly affect the computation of earnings, the presence of loan-loss reserve ratio supports the label "Earnings Growth". In 1986 and 1988 this variable alone forms a factor. Non-interest income aligns with earnings growth in 1987. The independent variables do not load consistently into this factor; nor is the factor significant in the model.

Dividend Payout

The dividend payout ratio (DIV) consistently formed a one variable factor in all years except 1988 when unpledged securities aligned with dividend payout ratio. The factor is called "Dividends" because even in 1988 the dividend payout ratio factor loading score was greater. This factor is not significant in any of the regression models.

Cash Demands

The ratio of demand deposits/total liabilities (D/L) provides a measure of a commercial bank's cash needs. This variable together with unpledged securities formed a factor in 1984. Since the factor loading score (.685) for D/L is greater than unpledged securities, the factor is named "cash demands." In 1985 demand deposits/total liabilities alone forms a factor. In 1986, 1987, and 1988 the ratio of federal funds sold/total assets aligns with the demand deposits ratio to form a factor. The relationship of these liquid assets to demand deposits is clear. A greater amount of deposits provides greater funds for short-term investments.

Summary of Factor Analysis

Ideally the factors should contain the same independent variables throughout all years examined. This did not occur. Since the method of computation is uniform throughout the period of study, explanation for the inconsistencies lies in some unobservable element influencing the variables. A minimum variance explained score of 1.0 or greater provided a criterion for the number of factors produced. The analyses produced eight (8) factors in each of the years examined.

Factor Regression

An OLS regression model of the following general type provides the principal basis for the models of common characteristics formed.

OBS/EA = FACTOR1 + FACTOR2 + FACTOR3 + FACTOR4 + FACTOR5 + FACTOR6 + FACTOR7 + FACTOR8

Factor regression results are presented in Appendix B Tables 14 through 17. The factors were regressed against each dependent variable for each year of the study. A discussion of the OLS regression of the factors follows. Table 7 provides a summary of the significant factors found in the regressions models for each of the dependent variables. It is these significant factors that provide the basis for the models of common characteristics as presented in Table 5 earlier in the chapter.

Table 7

Summary of Significant Factors In Regression Models by Year

Standby Letters of Credit
Liquid Assets 1984-1986,1988
Capital 1984-1988
Performance 1984, 1986-1988
Earnings Growth 1987,1988
Income Components 1986,1987
Cash Demands 1986
Dividends 1988
Excess Funds 1984, 1988

Letters of Credit
Liquid Assets 1984-1986,1988
Capital 1984-1988
Cash Demands 1984
Income Components 1987
Earnings Growth 1987

Interest Rate Swaps
Capital 1985-1988
Liquid Assets 1986-1988
Performance 1987,1988
Earnings Growth 1987,1988
Income Components 1987
Cash Demands 1986,1987

Loan Sales
Capital 1985,1986,1988
Liquid Assets 1985,1987,1988
Performance 1985
Earnings Growth 1987,1988
Cash Demands 1986,1987
Excess Cash 1984

Liquid Asset Measures
   The liquid asset factor, which is primarily cash, entered the regression model as a significant variable for each of the dependent

variables. The association between liquid assets and the four dependent variables may differ.

SLC transactions represent potential liabilities. Some standbys do not require cash for funding because of the way the obligations are met. The guaranteeing bank credits the borrower's account and debits loans receivable, thus simultaneously creating a demand deposit and a loan. In the event a credit enhancement standby requires actual funding to a third party, cash is necessary. The reported commitment on the Consolidated Asset and Liability (CALL) report does not distinguish between the two types of SLCs. Prudent managers would keep cash available for funding of potential liabilities. The negative association indicated in 1984 between liquid assets and SLC activity may suggest that less available cash stimulates more SLC transactions. However, examination of the variables comprising the factor in 1984 offers a more plausible explanation. Net interest income loaded with a negative loading score into the same factor with the highly liquid assets. Net interest income rather than liquid assets likely is driving the relationship to a negative association between the liquid assets and SLC transactions.

The statistical significance of liquid asset ratios for four of the five years, 1984, 1985, 1986, and 1988 in the LOC regression model indicates a need for ready cash in order to meet LOC commitments. This explanation agrees with the economic substance of LOC transactions. Letters of credit require immediate funding upon completion of the transaction and presentation of the appropriate documents.

The liquid asset factor appears to be a determinant of interest rate swap and loan sale activity as well. These OBS financial instruments are categorized as "market" instruments. The financial markets' perception of participating banks in OBS market instruments provides explanation of the association between liquid assets and loan sales and swaps.

Liquid assets represent daily liquidity. High ratios of liquid assets to total assets are desirable from a liquidity viewpoint; but these assets earn no or low yields. Proper liquidity management requires a delicate balance between sufficient cash to meet daily liquidity requirements and earning the highest possible yield.

For both SWAP and SALE transactions, the financial community's perception of the bank is important. Only those banks perceived as stable and able to meet its liquidity requirements-both short-term and long-term-will have the opportunity to participate in SWAP and SALE transactions.

In swap transactions the bank may be providing the "end" position, or it may serve as intermediary. In either case a customer entering into an interest rate swap transaction wants the bank to continue in business. For the first type of swap, the bank will cover the position. In the second case, the bank administers the swap agreement.

Loan sales can be participation of loans sold to other banks or securitization of assets. In participations the "lead" bank, the bank originating the loan, sells participations in its loan to "downstream" banks, i.e., those purchasing a part of the loan. The "downstream" banks are concerned about the "lead" bank's stability because the borrower is a customer of that bank. The "lead" bank continues to service the loan and maintain the client relationship with the borrower. Liquid assets provides one measure of stability of a commercial bank, i.e., its short-term liquidity.

Performance

The performance factor is a significant independent variable for SLCs in each year except 1985. In 1984, 1987, and 1988 the association is negative indicating that as performance declines bank managers seek alternative products to enhance revenue. This suggests increased risk-taking on the part of bank management in its attempts to increase earnings. However, the sign was positive rather than negative in 1986. Examination of the elements of the performance factor in 1986 offers an explanation. Return on assets (ROA) is negatively related to the underlying construct while loan-loss reserve (LL) is positively related. The reverse is true in other years. Bank closings in 1986 were at record levels. Industrywide, banks generated a negative return on assets in 1986.

The performance factor failed to enter the regression model for LOC activity. Two other measures of income, income components and earnings growth, were significant factors in 1987 alone. This evidence is insufficient to support an association of performance with LOC transactions. Inclusion of performance in the LOC common characteristics model is not warranted.

Neither was the performance factor consistently significant in determining SWAP activity. In 1987 and 1988 alone the performance factor shows a negative association with SWAP activity.

Significance of the performance factor in the regression model for SALE model occurred only in 1985. Therefore, this factor is not included as a common characteristic for banks engaging in SALE transactions.

Capital

Capital measurements make up the only factor consistently significant throughout the entire period of examination for SLCs. Surprisingly, the relationship is positive rather than negative.

This result is consistent with Goldberg and Lloyd-Davies [1985] who found that banks with assets in excess of $100 million do not adjust their capital ratios to allow for any increased risk as a result of SLC transactions. Koppenhaver [1987] also found binding capital requirements to have little or no affect upon the decision to issue off balance sheet guarantees. The premise that bankers may take greater risk in their desire to improve capital positions or that banks move into OBS activity to avoid regulatory constraints is not supported by the evidence of this study.

Scrutiny of the data indicates that most banks routinely operate at or near the minimum requirements. Since the banks are already at or near minimums, no further decline in capital ratios is possible without violating regulatory constraints. An increased activity in SLC, LOC, SWAP, or SALE would necessarily have to be either a positive association or no association since decreasing capital (on average) is not possible. The positive association of capital and SLC activity is explained by the necessity of an adequate capital position for a bank to engage in credit-enhancing SLCs.

Capital measurements also proved significant for all years examined for LOCs. This result indicates the necessity of an adequate capital position in order to have the opportunity to engage in LOC transactions.

Results of the factor regression also suggests a strong association between the level of capital and participation in SWAP transactions. Further, the association is positive which indicates that as capital ratios decline SWAP transactions decline and as capital ratios improve SWAP transactions increase. This is consistent with good banking management which would dictate a solid capital base before participating in potentially risky transactions. It is also consistent with the idea that the financial community's perception of a bank's stability must be positive for that bank to have the opportunity to engage in SWAP and SALE transactions.

Capital measures were positively significant variables for SALE for the years 1985, 1986, and 1988. These results warrant the inclusion of the capital factor as a common characteristic of banks participating in loan sales.

There are three well-recognized measures of a bank's size-its total assets, demand deposits, and capital. Capital measures represent a bank's capacity to do business because they provide a measure of solvency risk. The economic net worth of a bank is the difference between market value of its assets and liabilities. Capital risk refers to the potential decrease in asset values before economic net worth becomes zero. A bank with higher capital can absorb more decrease in asset value than a bank with capital equal to a lower percent of assets.

Capital was the only factor consistently significant in the regression models for each of the dependent variables. This supports the anonymous quotation "Capital is everything." The bank will not attract customers seeking financial instruments unless it possesses a minimum base of resources with which to conduct business. This fact, taken with the observation that banks routinely operate at regulatory minimums, explains the positive association of the capital measures factor to each of the OBS instruments of this study.

Non-significant Factors

The ratio of demand deposits/total liabilities served as a surrogate for cash demands. The cash demand factor entered the regression model for SALE sporadically. This result is consistent with the *a-priori* assumption that loan sale activity increases as cash needs increase. Liquidating loans provides ready cash. Sufficient evidence does not exist to include cash demand as a common characteristic of banks engaging in SLCs, LOCs, SWAPs or SALEs.

The traditional accounting liquidity measures of current ratio and quick ratio did not enter any of the regression models as a significant variable. After making the computations from the database, it became apparent that the two ratios are nearly the same because current assets for a commercial bank are highly liquid. The cash demand factor provided a more meaningful measure of liquidity.

The dividend payout ratio was not a significant factor in any of the regression models. During this time period, the commercial banking industry experienced high losses and multiple failures. Many banks failed to pay any dividends. Apparently, survival was such an issue that maintenance of a consistent dividend payout ratio was inconsequential.

Income components entered the SLC regression model in 1986 and 1987 and the LOC and SWAP models for 1987. This result is not sufficiently consistent to establish a pattern of significance in the models. Income components is not included as a common characteristic of banks engaging in any of the four types of OBS transactions.

Earnings growth displayed sporadic significance in the regression models, but no consistent pattern emerged. In 1987 and 1988 there was a negative association between earnings growth and SLC and SWAP. In 1987 there was a negative association between earnings growth and LOC and SALE. These results do not justify the inclusion of this factor in the final model.

The factor including federal funds sold was not significant in any of the regression models. This factor is not part of the final model.

SUBSAMPLES

Throughout the study size behaved more like a covariant than an independent variable. In the factor analysis SIZE either aligned with the capital measures or fragmented across the factors. A subsample of banks having assets in excess of $5 billion was partitioned for further study. The statistical procedures performed on this subsample duplicated the procedures performed on the full sample. Results from the factor regression support the inclusion of the same variables identified for the general sample in a model of common characteristics on banks having assets of $5 billion or greater that participate in OBS transactions involving SLCs, LOCs, SWAPs, and SALEs. These variables were capital and liquid assets for all of the dependent variables and performance for SLCs.

A further subsample defining the population as those banks having assets of $10 billion or greater was partitioned from the full sample. Valid factor analysis could not be performed on this group because the number of variables exceeded the number of observations. An OLS regression procedure was performed on the original independent variables. The resulting models were free of multicollinearity according to statistical diagnostics. However, logically the nature of the independent variables indicates some correlation is present. This information is, therefore, not considered in the determination of the model of common characteristics. The results of the analyses of the full sample form the basis for conclusions regarding the hypotheses.

CONCLUSIONS

Seven initial hypotheses are presented with regard to the common characteristics of banks having OBS transactions. Refer to Chapter Four for an explanation of these hypotheses. These seven hypotheses are restated here into six hypotheses accommodating the factors as independent variables.

H1: There will be a positive association between a firm's performance and the firm's use of SLCs, LOCs, SWAPs, and SALEs.

H2: There will be a positive association between a firm's capital and the firm's use of SLCs, LOCs, SWAPS, and SALEs.

H3: There will be a positive association between a firm's liquid assets and the firm's activity in SLCs, LOCs, SWAPs, and SALEs.

H4: There will be a negative association between a firm's cash demands and the firm's activity in SLCs, LOCs, SWAPs, and SALEs.

H5: There will be a positive association between a firm's income components, earnings growth, and dividend payout ratio and the firm's activity in SLCs, LOCs, SWAPs, and SALEs.

H6: There will be a positive association between the firm's liquidity measures of current ratio and quick ratio and the firm's activity in SLCs, LOCs, SWAPs, and SALEs.

Table 8 presents each of the hypotheses and the outcomes of the analyses. One of three outcomes is possible-the null hypotheses is rejected; the null hypothesis is accepted; or there is no relationship.

Table 8

Summary of Outcomes Relative to Hypotheses

Hypothesis	SLC	LOC	SWAP	SALE
H1	Reject	N/R	N/R	N/R
H2	Accept	Accept	Accept	Accept
H3	Accept	Accept	Accept	Accept
H4	N/R	N/R	N/R	N/R
H5	N/R	N/R	N/R	N/R
H6	N/R	N/R	N/R	N/R

N/R indicates no relationship.

Subjective judgment decided which factors to include in the model of common characteristics. A number of criteria were considered in making the decision. First, the factor must have been a significant independent variable in the regression model for the dependent variable. Second, the factor must have been significant in the model for a majority of the years studied. Finally, the factor included in the model must be sensible, i.e., the relationship should not be an anomaly of the statistical procedures.

As the table shows the null hypothesis is rejected for H1 for SLCs. Performance is negatively related to the use of SLCs. There is no relationship between performance and the other dependent variables.

The null hypotheses two and three are accepted for all of the dependent variables. Both liquid assets and capital prove to be positively associated with all of the dependent variables. Each of the other hypotheses (H4-H6) show no relationship to the dependent variables.

The statistical analyses provided support for the inclusion of certain factors in models of common characteristics of banks engaging in standby letters of credit, letters of credit, interest rate swaps, and loan sales. A summary of these models is presented in Table 9.

Table 9

Model Comparison by Financial Instrument

SLC	LOC	SWAP	SALE
Performance	**		
Capital	**	**	****
Liquid Assets	**	**	****

**Common characteristic in the model for this dependent variable.

The determinants for standby letters of credit and letters of credit, the financial instruments categorized as credit instruments are similar but not identical. The analyses of LOC data does not support the inclusion of performance as a common characteristic. The availability of liquid assets and sufficient business capacity as evidenced by capital are determinants of SLC, LOC, SWAP, and SALE transactions.

Implications, limitations, and suggestions for future research of this subject are presented in Chapter Seven.

VII

Contributions, Implications, Limitations, Suggestions For Future Research

This chapter describes the contributions of the research to the finance and accounting body of knowledge and its implications to various groups. Limitations of the study and suggestions for future research are also discussed.

CONTRIBUTIONS

This research contributes to the accounting body of knowledge in several areas. First, it extends the positive accounting theory hypotheses of Watts and Zimmerman [1986] to a previously unexamined industry. The study tests the bonus plan hypothesis, the debt/equity hypothesis, and the size hypothesis in commercial banking. No support was found for any of these hypotheses. Offsetting the Watts and Zimmerman size, i.e., political costs theory, are regulatory considerations which encourage banks to become large entities. Commercial banks typically operate with large sums of debt; however, the primary creditors of a commercial bank are its depositors. Unlike holders of long-term debt, depositors are not concerned with transfers of wealth to stockholders because they are protected by Federal Deposit Insurance Corporation (FDIC) insurance coverage. Regulatory constraints focus upon a bank's having sufficient equity. The study showed that debt/equity ratio functions as an equity measure in commercial banking. The percentage of stock owned by directors and officers as a group was minimal (usually less than 1 percent). Any agency issues which may exist in commercial banking are manifested differently from the relationships depicted in Watts and Zimmerman's [1986] positive accounting theory hypotheses.

Liquidity variables, which have not been previously tested in positive accounting choice studies, were included in the present study.

These included short-term asset and liability liquidity measures. Specifically, the asset liquidity variables not used in previous studies are Cratio, Ibratio, Ffratio, and Unpsec. (See table 4 for a definition of these variables.) The measures for short-term asset liquidity proved to be significant in predicting OBS transactions for SLCs, LOCs, SWAPs, and SALEs. The independent variable DL measured short-term liability liquidity. Contrary to expectations, cash demands, measured by DL, are not determinants of the OBS decision.

A number of studies have made empirical investigations of standby letters of credit [Koppenhaver 1987, Bennett 1987, James 1988, Goldberg and Lloyd-Davies 1985, Rose 1989], and loan sales [James 1988, Pavel and Phillis 1987]. The present research extends that work through the use of additional variables and a differently-defined population. The independent variables introduced in this study were the measures of liquid assets, namely, Cratio, Ibratio, Ffratio, and Unpsec. Other variables not previously used include DE, DO, EARG, and DIV, ROA, ROE, Current, and Quick. (See table 4 for definition of these variables.)

This project defined its population as domestic banks having total assets equal to or greater than $300 million. These parameters had not been applied to previous studies of financial instruments. Eliminating those banks unlikely to participate in off balance sheet (OBS) transactions allows the study to concentrate on examination of characteristics of those banks actively participating in the OBS market. The statistical findings are not influenced by banks excluded by financial markets from using sophisticated financial instrument transactions.

No empirical studies of interest rate swaps or commercial letters of credit hade been published to date. Previous research in this area was limited to analytical analysis. The present research establishes an association between capital and liquid assets and both swaps and loan sales.

IMPLICATIONS

The presence of OBS transactions create situations of information asymmetry. For the period researched only limited disclosure requirements existed. SFAS No. 5 covers contingencies and commitments and specifically requires disclosure of obligations of commercial banks under standby letters of credit. The standard does not include commercial letters of credit and similar instruments where the issuing bank expects the beneficiary to draw upon the issuer and which do not "guaranty" payment of money or obligation.

Some entities are required by the Securities Exchange Commission (SEC) or regulators of their particular industry to make some disclosure of financial instruments. Other firms have voluntarily disclosed OBS activity either in notes to the financial statements or more frequently management discussion and analysis. Because of the absence of uniform disclosure requirements, comparability among financial statements is not possible.

The disclosure requirements for commercial banks by the Federal Reserve System and FDIC made certain information regarding banks OBS activities available in the banks' Consolidated Asset and Liability (CALL) reports. While these CALL reports can be made available for public consumption, there is little evidence that the information on these reports is widely known. First, the seeker of the information must be sufficiently knowledgeable about banking reporting requirements to know the information exists. Many individual investors doubtless are not. Financial analysts who follow the banking industry presumably would be aware of the disclosure requirements for the industry. However, conversation with one of the leading suppliers of banking financial information revealed that the primary subscribers to their information service are commercial banks, large accounting firms, and investment bankers. This does not preclude the possibility, however, that analysts obtain the information directly from the FDIC. Since that is one of the most expensive and least efficient sources to use, it appears unlikely that many analysts would pursue information from the FDIC.

The efficient market hypothesis in the semi-strong form is based on the premise that all publicly available information is impounded quickly into market price. With information asymmetry as in the case of OBS transactions, the market equilibrium that is achieved may not be an appropriate measure of a share's true worth based upon risk and return. The market cannot assimilate risks that are not publicly known into the share price. Knowledge of the common characteristics of firms engaging in OBS activities should provide useful clues for appropriate assessment of risk by investors, creditors, analysts, regulators. Such knowledge may offer insight into the motivation for using OBS instruments.

Statement of Financial Accounting Standards (SFAS) No. 105, which applies to all entities including commercial banks, requires disclosure of "all financial instruments with off-balance-sheet risk of accounting loss and all financial instruments with concentrations of credit risk except those specifically excluded.."[FASB, 1990]. SFAS No. 105's requirements, cover the four financial instruments of this study, but the requirements did not become effective until reporting periods following June 15, 1990. SFAS No. 105's disclosure requirements does much to ameliorate information asymmetry resulting from OBS transactions, but it does not eliminate it. As stated in Chapter One the purpose of this research has been to form a model of common characteristics of banks that participate in OBS activity.

Perhaps the group that can most benefit from an awareness of which firms are likely to be active in OBS markets are accounting policy makers. The FASB struggled to achieve a disclosure standard acceptable to its constituency which provides relevant information to third-party users of financial statements. The process included numerous hearings, two exposure drafts, and a delay of the intended effective date.

The second phase of the FASB's project, measurement and recognition, is even more complex. In today's environment of constantly changing instruments, this second phase may be impossible to achieve. Full disclosure of all relevant aspects of OBS activities may be the most appropriate approach to the problem. Associating firm characteristics to OBS activity, may allow the FASB to "get a handle on" actual risks for each OBS financial instrument.

A model of common characteristics should help the Board evaluate the necessity of the measurement and recognition phase of its OBS project and other future considerations. The models for LOCs, SWAPs, and SALEs indicate that determinants of OBS transactions are more likely to be driven by market stimuli rather than declining financial strength. However, the negative association of performance with SLCs supports the notion of aggressive risk-taking to augment revenue.

LIMITATIONS

This study uses commercial banks with assets greater than $300 million as a population. Commercial banking is a highly regulated industry that provides a social good which is necessary for the operation of a capital-market based economy. These factors make it impossible to generalize any results of this study beyond the commercial banking industry. Because certain characteristics of a commercial bank are dependent upon its size, the results cannot be generalized to banks smaller than the population of the study ($300 million or greater in assets). Because of differing economic consequences of the various financial instruments, no assumption can be made that the findings of this study apply to other financial instruments.

Results of the study then are industry specific and financial instrument specific. No generalizations should be made outside commercial banking. No generalizations should be made to banks smaller than $300 million. No generalizations should be made to involvement in financial instruments other than SLCs, LOCs, SWAPs, and SALEs.

Finally, recognition must be given to the reliability of the database. The financial information upon which this study was based was drawn from magnetic tapes of CALL reports as submitted to the FDIC. Several areas of error are possible. First, the information submitted to the FDIC may be in error or incomplete. The information is subject to audit, but 100 percent of CALL reports are not examined. Second, the information is transferred to the magnetic tapes. Whether this is done manually or by machine scanning errors can occur, particularly errors of omission. Third, transforming the raw data to a SAS dataset, the database for this research, may result in errors.

To overcome the question of reliability in the data, certain key figures of a selected group of banks were compared to *Moody's Bank & Finance Manual*. No differences were noted between the financial data reported in *Moody's* and that reported on the CALL report. OBS information is not reported in *Moody's* so it could not be verified. The assumption was made that if other financial information agreed then the OBS information was also correct. This verification procedure was performed for a very limited number of banks in the sample.

SUGGESTIONS FOR FUTURE RESEARCH

The most important future project is to extend the study. Major events impacting disclosure of OBS financial instruments and regulatory constraints have occurred and are continuing to occur. These events are the effective date of FAS No. 105, the advent of risk-based capital, and most recently the elimination of primary capital. As part of its movement to risk-based capital, the FDIC eliminated primary capital January, 1991, replacing it with tier-one capital. The significance of this is the disallowance of loan loss reserves as part of tier-one capital.

The requirements of FAS No. 105 are effective for reporting years after June 15, 1990. Risk-based capital requirements were phased in and became completely effective in 1992. A study comparing common characteristics of commercial banks having OBS transactions after either or both of those events with the present study should provide much insight into whether transactions are chosen because they are off the balance sheet or if these transactions are off the balance sheet because accounting principles have not kept pace with the economic environment.

An extension of the present study to other financial instruments which are not reported on the balance sheet would give information as to the breadth of OBS instruments. This could answer questions about banks choices of transactions.

A case-study type project with the instruments themselves under detailed scrutiny would provide much information about how these transactions are structured. The question to be answered would be whether the transaction is off the balance sheet because of structure changes to avoid disclosure and recognition requirements or because accounting principles have not adequately addressed the accounting issues of the transactions.

A pilot study of a selected number of banks verifying all financial information found on the FDIC tapes would provide comfort in the validity of the FDIC tapes as a database. Sources of information such as *Moody's Bank & Finance Manual*, the banks' registrations with Securities and Exchange Commission, proxy statements, and annual reports could provide information on most of the items in the CALL report. For those items reported only on the CALL report, verification could be made though direct communication with banks.

APPENDIX A

Table 10

Standby Letters of Credit
Credit Enhancement

Issuing SLC Account Party *(Customer)*	*Bank*	Beneficiary (accepts contract with account party *based on SLC*
Seeks SLC Pays fee →	Notifies Beneficiary →	Accepts Contract
In Event of Default		← Presents SLC
	Pays Beneficiary →	
	Presents SLC for collection to ← account party	
Pays bank →		

Table 11

Commercial Letters of Credit

Buyer	*Banks*	*Seller*
Concludes sales contract providing for payment by LOC	←	→
Instructs bank to issue LOC in favor of seller→		
	Contacts bank in seller's country to confirm/advise	
	Advising/confirming bank informs seller LOC issued	
		←Ships Goods
		←Sends documentation
	Checks documents against LOC terms sends to issuing bank (1) pays sellers (2)→	
	Issuing bank checks documents (1) pays confirming bank (1)	
	confirming bank pays seller→	

(1) Assumes advising/confirming bank
(2) No advising/confirming bank

Interest Rate Swap

The example presented in Table 12 of the basic structure of an interest rate swap is slightly modified from one presented by Turnbull [1987]. Firm A can issue U.S. dollar-denominated fixed-rate debt at 10.75%, or it can issue floating-rate debt at London Interbank Offered Rate (LIBOR) plus 25 basis points (bps). Firm B has a lower credit rating than Firm A, and it must pay 11.7% on fixed-rate debt of the same maturity or floating-rate debt at LIBOR plus 37.5 bps. Firm B would like to issue fixed debt but with lower interest rates. Firm A prefers to issue floating-rate debt because it provides a better fit in its overall portfolio management. The differential in the fixed-term market is 95 bps, but in the floating-rate market the differential is only 12.5 bps. The net differential of 82.5 bps represents the gain from the swap that is divided among the swap participants. Firm A issues fixed debt at 10.75%, and firm B issues floating rate debt at LIBOR plus 37.5%. Firm A agrees to pay the financial intermediary a floating rate of LIBOR plus 15 bps, and the financial intermediary pays A a fixed rate of 11%. Firm B agrees to pay the financial intermediary a fixed rate of 11.1% and the financial intermediary pays B a floating rate of LIBOR plus 10 bps. Firm A's net payment is LIBOR less 10 bps. Firm B has issued floating debt at LIBOR plus 37.5% and has a net payment of a fixed rate of 11.375%. In effect Firm A has issued floating rate debt at LIBOR less 10 bps, and firm B has effectively issued fixed-rate debt at 11.375%. Firm A has saved 35 bps via the swap over what it would have paid to issue floating-rate debt directly. Firm B has effectively issued fixed-rate debt at 11.375%. If it had issued fixed-rate directly, Firm B would have had to pay 11.7% interest. Firm B saved 32.5 bps. The financial intermediary gains 10 bps on the fixed swap and 5 bps on the floating swap.

Table 12
Interest Rate Swap Illustrated

Firm A	Intermediary	Firm B
floating LIBOR + 15bps→		←Fixed 11.1%

←fixed 11%		Floating LIBOR + 10bps→
↓		↓
Issues fixed		Issues
at 10.75%		floating
		LIBOR + 37.5

	Firm A	Firm B
Pays debtholders	10./75%	LIBOR +37.5bps
To Intermediary	LIBOR+ 15bps	11.1%
Receives from		
Intermediary	11.0%	Libor +10bps
Net Payment	LIBOR-10bps	11.375%

RESULT:

**A has effectively issued floating rate debt at LIBOR -10bps

**B has effectively issued fixed rate debt at 11.375%

**A saves 35 bps.

**B saves 32.5bps over direct fixed rate

**Financial intermediary gains 10 bps on fixed rate debt

**Financial intermediary gains 5bps on floating rate debt

Table 13

Loan Sale Funds Flow

Borrower	*Bank*	*Purchaser*
	←Makes Loan	
	Sells Loan	←
Pays Bank→		
	Pays Purchaser less servicing fee→	

APPENDIX B

Table 14

Standby Letters of Credit
Factor Regression Results

	1984	1985	1986	1987	1988
Intercept	.0255	.0305	.0279	.0264	.0293
	.0001	.0001	.0001	.0001	.0001
Performance-	.0099		.0036	-.0064	-.0069
	.0001		.0079	.0002	.0001
Capital	.0172	.0264	.0156	.0139	.0153
	.0001	.0001	.0001	.0001	.0001
Liquid	-.0099	.0071	.0091		.0082
Assets	.0001	.0019	.0001		.0001
Earnings				-.0140	-.0093
Growth				.0001	.0001
Income			-.0036	-.0405	
Components			.0071	.0001	
Cash Demands-			.0034		
			.0125		
Dividend					-.0061
					.0001
Excess Funds	.0036				.0034
	.0239				.0212
R-SQUARE	E.3963	.3032	.3885	.7115	.4469
F VALUE	54.327	71.568	40.907	181.876	37.705
PROB >F	.0001	.0001	.0001	.0001	.0001

All variables in the model are significant at the .1000 level. No other variables met the .05 significance level for entry into the model.

Table 15

Letters of Credit
Factor Regression Results

	1984	1985	1986	1987	1988
Intercept	.0055	.0063	.0059	.0061	.0063
	.0001	.0001	.0001	.0001	.0001
Liquid Assets	-.0143	.0016	.0033		.0026
	.0001	.0230	.0001		.0002
Capital	.0034	.0045	.0018	.0028	.0031
	.0001	.0001	.0079	.0008	.0001
Cash Demand	.0017				
	.0097				
Income Components				.0081	
				.0001	
Earnings Growth				-.0031	
				.0003	
R-SQUARE	.6118	.1201	.0863	.2864	.1077
F- VALUE	177.541	22.445	15.340	39.604	17.146
PROB>F	.0001	.0001	.0001	.0001	.0001

All variables in the model are significant at the .1000 level. No other variables met the .05 significance level for entry into the model.

Table 16

Interest Rate Swaps
Factor Regression Results

	1985	1986	1987	1988
Intercept	.0158	.0389	.0407	.0772
	.0001	.0003	.0001	.0001
Performance			-.0258	-.0350
			.0009	.0104
Capital	.0269	.0346	.0974	.1393
	.0001	.0012	.0001	.0001
Liquid Assets		.0213	.0180	.0395
		.0448	.0198	.0039
Earnings Growth			-.0353	-.1439
			.0001	.0001
Income Components			.1437	
			.0001	
Cash Demand		-.0292	-.0444	
		.0061	.0001	
R-SQUARE	.2450	.0646	.6646	.4521
F VALUE	107.369	7.456	97.763	58.175
PROB >F	.0001	.00013	.0001	.0001

All variables in the model are significant at the .1000 level. No other variable met the .05 significance level for entry into the model.

Table 17

Loan Sales
Factor Regression Results

	1984	1985	1986	1987	1988
Intercept	.0219	.0200	.0286	.1088	.0215
	.0004	.0001	.0011	.2213	.0001
Cash Demands			.0433	.4546	
			.0001	.0001	
Capital		.0095	.0219		.0141
		.0012	.0125		.0003
Liquid Assets		.0063		.1818	.0120
		.0310		.0417	.0121
Performance		.0059			
		.0437			
Earnings Growth				.2096	-.0335
				.0150	.0001
Excess Cash	.0131	.0067			
	.0332	.0208			
R-SQUARE	.0133	.0728	.0873	.1081	.2564
F-VALUE	4.571	6.230	15.540	11.959	32.527
PROB > F	.0332	.0001	.0001	.0001	.0001

All variables in the model are significant at the .1000 level. No other variable met the .05 significance level for entry into the model.

BIBLIOGRAPHY

Andrews, Suzanna and Henny Sender. "Off Balance Sheet
Risk:Where Is It Leading the Banks?" *Institutional Investor*
(January 1986), pp. 75-84.

Arak, Marcelle, Arturo Estrella, Laurie Goodman, and Andrew
Silver. "Interest Rate Swaps: An Alternative Explanation."
Financial Management (Summer 1988), pp. 12-18.

Ayres, Frances L. "Characteristics of Firms Electing Early
Adoption of SFAS 52." *Journal of Accounting and
Economics* (June 1986), pp. 143-158.

Beaver, W. H., R. Clarke, and W. F. Wright. "The Association
between Unsystematic Security Returns and the Magnitude
of Earnings Forecast Errors." *Journal of Accounting
Research* (Autumn 1979), pp. 316-340.

Beaver, W., P. Kettler, and M. Scholes. "The Association
Between Market-Determined and Accounting-Determined
Risk Measures." *The Accounting Review* (October 1970),
pp. 654-682.

Bennett, Barbara. "Off Balance Sheet Risk in Banking: The Case
of Standby Letters of Credit. *Economic Review* 1 (Winter
1986), pp. 19-29.

Bicksler, James and Andrew Chen. " An Economic Analysis of
Interest Rate Swaps." *The Journal of Finance* (July 1986),
pp. 645-655.

Boland, Lawrence A. and Irene Gordon. "Criticizing Positive
Accounting Theory." *Contemporary Accounting Research*
(Fall 1992), pp. 142-170.

Bowen, R. M., E. W. Noreen, and J.M. Lacey. "The
Determinants of the Corporate Decision to Capitalize

Interest. *"Journal of Accounting and Economics* (August 1981), pp. 151-179.

Bowman, R. "The Theoretical Relationship Between Systematic Risk and Financial Accounting Variables." *The Journal of Finance* (July 1979), pp. 617-630.

Brearley, Richard and Stewart Myers. *Principles of Corporate Finance.* New York: McGraw-Hill Book Company, 1984.

Brewer, E., G. Koppenhaver, and D. Wilson. "The Market Perception of Bank Off Balance Sheet Activities." *Proceedings of a Conference on Bank Structure and Competition.* Chicago: Federal Reserve Bank, 1986.

Brewer, Elijah. "The Risks of Banks Expanding Their Permissible Nonbanking Activities." *Financial Review* (November 1990), pp. 517-537.

Brewer, Elijah, and G.D. Koppenhaver. "The Impact of Standby Letters of Credit on Bank Risk: A Note." *Journal of Banking and Finance.* (December 1992), pp. 1037-1046.

Brigham, Eugene F. and Louis C. Gapenski. *Financial Management Theory and Practice* Chicago: The Dryden Press, 1988.

Bryan, Lowell L. "The Credit Bomb in Our Financial System." *Harvard Business Review* (January-February 1987), pp. 45-51.

Cates, David C. and Henry A. Davis. *Off-Balance Sheet Banking and the Changing Nature of Financial Risk.* New York: Robert Morris Associates, 1987.

Cecchetti, Stephen G. "High Real Interest Rates: Can They Be Explained?" *Economic Review* (September-October 1986), pp. 31-41.

Chambers, A. E. and S. H. Penman. "Timeliness of Reporting
Stock Price Reaction to Earnings Announcements." *Journal
of Accounting Research* (Spring 1984), pp. 21-47.

Comiskey, Eugene E., Ruth Ann McEwen, and Charles W.
Mulford. "A Test of Pro Forma Consolidation of Finance
Subsidiaries." *Financial Management* (August 1987),
pp. 45-50.

Daley, Lane. A. and R. L. Vigeland. "The Effects of Debt
Covenants and Political Costs on the Choice of Accounting
Methods: The Case of Accounting for R & D Cost."*Journal
of Accounting and Economics* (December 1983), pp. 195-
211.

DeAngelo, Linda E. "Managerial Competition, Information Costs,
and Corporate Governance." *Journal of Accounting and
Economics* 11 (January 1988), pp. 3-36.

Deakin, Edward B. "Rational Economic Behavior and Lobbying on
Accounting Issues: Evidence from the Oil and Gas
Industry." *The Accounting Review* (January 1989), pp. 137-
151.

Dhaliwal, Dan S. "The Effect of the Firm's Capital Structure on
the Choice of Accounting Methods." *The Accounting
Review.* (January 1980), pp. 78-84.

Dhaliwal, Dan., Gerald L. Salamon, and Dan Smith. "The Effect
of Owner Versus Management Control on the Choice of
Accounting Methods." *Journal of Accounting and
Economics* 4 (July 1982), pp. 41-53.

Diamond, Douglas. "Financial Intermediation and Delegated
Monitoring." *Review of Economic Studies* (July 1984), pp.
393-414.

El-Gazzar, Samir, Steven Lilien, and Victor Pastena. "The Use of
Off=Balance-Sheet Financing to Circumvent Financial

Covenant Restrictions." *Journal of Accounting Auditing and Finance* (Spring 1989), pp. 217-231.

El-Gazzar, Samir, Steven Lilien, and Victor Pastena. "Accounting for Leases by Lessees." *Journal of Accounting and Economics* (October 1986), pp. 217-237.

Ernst & Whinney. *Off-Balance Sheet Financing Arrangements in Banks and Bank Holding Companies.* Cleveland: Ernst & Whinney, 1986.

Fama, E. F. "Agency Problems and the Theory of the Firm." Journal of Political Economy (April 1980), pp. 288-307.

Federal Banking Law Reporter. Chicago: Commerce Clearing House, 1990.

Filler, Richard. "Credit Risks and Costs in Interest Rate Swaps." *Journal of Cash Management* (January/February 1993) pp. 38-41.

Financial Accounting Standards Board. *Accounting Standards Current Text General Standards as of June 1, 1989.* Norwalk: Financial Accounting Standards Board, 1989.

Financial Accounting Standards Board. *Disclosure of Information about Financial Instruments with Concentrations of Credit Risk.* Norwalk: Financial Accounting Standards Board, 1989.

Financial Accounting Standards Board. *Disclosure of Information about Financial Instruments with Off-Balance-Sheet Risk and Financial Instruments with Concentrations of Credit Risk.* Norwalk: Financial Accounting Standards Board, 1990.

Financial Accounting Standards Board. *EITF Abstracts A Summary of the Proceedings of the FASB Emerging Issues Task Force.* Norwalk: Financial Accounting Standards Board, 1989.

Flannery, Mark and Christopher James. "The Effect of Interest Rate Changes on the Common Stock Returns of Financial Institutions." *Journal of Finance* (September 1984), pp. 1141-1153.

Fogler, Russell H. and Sundaram Ganapathy. *Financial Econometrics for Researchers in Finance and Accounting.* Englewood Cliffs, N. J.: Prentice-Hall, 1982.

Funk, G. "Letters of Credit: U.C.C. Article 5 and the Uniform Customs and Practices." *Banking Law Journal* (October 1982), pp. 1035-1037.

Goldberg, Michael A. and Peter R. Lloyd-Davies. "Standby Letters of Credit: Are Banks Overextending Themselves?" *Journal of Bank Research* (Spring 1985), pp. 28-39.

Gorton, Gary B. and Joseph G. Haubrich. "Bank Deregulation, Credit Markets and the Control of Capital." *Carnegie-Rochester Conference Series on Public Policy 26* 1986.

Gorton, Gary and George Pennacchi. "Are Loan Sales Really Off-Balance-Sheet?" *Journal of Accounting Auditing and Finance* (Spring 1989), pp. 125-145.

Gregorash, George and Theresa Ford. "Banking 1987: A Year of Reckoning." *Economic Perspectives.* (July-August 1988), pp. 3-13.

Hagerman, R. L. and M. Zmijewski. "Some Economic Determinants of Accounting Policy." *Journal of Accounting and Economics.* (August 1979), pp. 141-161.

Hamada, R. "The Effects of the Firm's Capital Structure on the Systematic Risk of Common Stocks." *The Journal of Finance* (May 1972), pp. 435-452.

Hassan, M. Rabin. "Capital Market Tests of Risk Exposure of Loan Sale Activities of Large U.S. Commercial Banks."

Quarterly Journal of Business and Economics (Winter 1993) pp. 27-49.

Healy, Paul M. "The Effect of Bonus Schemes on Accounting Decisions." *Journal of Accounting and Economics*. 7 (April 1985), pp. 85-123.

Hindley, Brian. "Separation of Ownership and Control in the Modern Corporation." *Journal of Law and Economics* (April 1970), pp. 185-221.

Houlihan, William A. and Ashwinpaul C. Sondhi. "DeFacto Capitalization of Operating Leases: The Effect on Debt Capacity." *Corporate Accounting* (Summer 1984), pp. 3-13.

Jackson, Barbara Bund. *Multivariate Data Analysis*, Homewood, Ill.: Richard D. Irwin, Inc., 1983.

James, Christopher. "Off-Balance-Sheet Activities and the Underinvestment Problem in Banking." *Journal of Accounting Auditing and Finance* (Spring 1989), pp. 111-124.

James, Christopher. "The Use of Loan Sales and Standby Letters of Credit by Commercial Banks."Working Paper, University of Oregon, 1987.

James, Christopher. "The Use of Loan Sales and Standby Letters of Credit by Commercial Banks." *Journal of Monetary Economics* 22 (November 1988), pp. 395-422.

Jensen, M. C. and W. H. Meckling. "Theory of the Firm: Managerial Behavior, Agency Costs and Ownership Structure." *Journal of Financial Economics* (October 1976), pp. 305-360.

Johnson, Frank P. "A Glossary of Ratios for Bank Auditors." *Bank Accounting and Finance* (January 1989): 52-56.

Johnston, John. *Econometric Methods*. New York: McGraw Hill Company, 1972.

Kalay, A. "Stockholder-Bondholder Conflict and Dividend Constraints." *Journal of Accounting and Economics* (July 1982), pp. 211-233.

Kelly, Lauren. "Corporate Management Lobbying on FAS No. 8: Some Further Evidence," *Journal of Accounting Research* 23 (Autumn 1985), pp. 619-632.

Khambata, Dara. "Off-Balance-Sheet Activities of U.S. Banks: An Empirical Evaluation." *Columbia Journal of World Business* (Summer 1989) pp. 3-13

Koch, Timothy W, *Bank Management*. New York: The Dryden Press, 1988.

Koppenhaver, G. "Standby Letters of Credit." *Economic Perspectives*. Chicago: Federal Reserve Bank, 1987.

Koppenhaver, G.D. and Roger Stover. "Standby Letters of Credit and Large Bank Capital: An Empirical Analysis." *Journal of Banking and Finance* (April 1991), pp. 315-327.

Leftwich, R. "Accounting Information in Private Markets: Evidence from Private Lending Agreements." *The Accounting Review* (January 1983), pp. 23-42.

"Evidence of the Impact of Mandatory Changes in Accounting Principles on Corporate Loan Agreements." *Journal of Accounting and Economics* (March 1981), pp. 3-36.

Leftwich, R. and R. Holthausen. "The Economic Consequences of Accounting Choice: Evidence from Private Lending Agreements." *Journal of Accounting and Economics* (August 1983), pp. 77-117.

Lereah, David. "The Growth of Interest Rate Swaps." *The Bankers Magazine* (May-June 1986), pp. 36-41.

Lilien, Steven and Victor Pastena. "Determinants of Intramethod Choice in the Oil and Gas Industry." *Journal of Accounting and Economics* 4 (December 1982), pp. 145-170.

Mendenhall, William and Terry Sincich. *A Second Course Business Statistics*. San Francisco: Dellen Publishing Company, 1986.

Merton, Robert C. "On the Pricing of Corporate Debt: The Risk Structure of Interest Rates." *The Journal of Finance* 29 (May 1974), pp. 449-470.

Millard, Neal S. and Brian Semkow. "The New Risk-Based Capital Framework and Its Application to Letters of Credit." *Banking Law Journal* (November/December 1989) pp. 500-514.

Modigliani, F. and M. H. Miller. "The Cost of Capital, Corporation Finance and the Theory of Investment." *American Economic Review* (June 1958), pp. 261-297.

Modigliani, F. and M. H. Miller. "Corporate Income Taxes and the Cost of Capital: A Correction." *American Economic Review* (June 1966), pp. 333-391.

Monsen, Joseph, Jr. and Anthony Downs. "The Theory of Large Managerial Firms." *Journal of Political Economy* (June 1965), pp. 221-236.

Moulton, Janice M. "Nonbank Banks: Catalyst for Interstate Banking." *Business Review* (November-December 1985), pp. 3-18.

Myers, Stewart C. "Determinants of Corporate Borrowing." *Journal of Financial Economics* 5 (November 1977), pp. 147-175.

Nance, Deana R., C.W. Smith, Jr. and C.W. Smithson. "The Determinants of Corporate Hedging." Working paper, University of North Texas, 1989.

Noreen, Eric. "An Empirical Comparison of Probit and OLS Regression Hypothesis Tests," *Journal of Accounting Research* 26 (Spring 1988), pp. 119-133.

Pawlowic, Dean. "Standby Letters of Credit: Review and Update." *Uniform Commercial Code Law Journal* (Spring 1991) pp. 391-419.

Patell, J. M. and M. S. Wolfson. "Good News, Bad News, and the Intraday Timing of Corporate Disclosures." *Accounting Review* (July 1982), pp. 509-527.

Paton, W. A. and A. C. Littleton. *An Introduction to Corporate Accounting Standards*. Sarasota: American Accounting Association, 1940.

Pavel, Christine and David Phillis. "Why Commercial Banks Sell loans: An Empirical Analysis." *Economic Perspectives* 14 (July-August 1988), pp. 16-31.

Peltzman, S. "Toward a More General Theory of Regulation." *Journal of Law and Economics* (August 1976), pp. 211-240.

"Private Survey Tracks Executive Compensation." *Journal of Accountancy* (July 1987), p. 39.

Pruden, Thomas E. "Discover What Is Changing In Bank Credit Agreements." *Corporate Cashflow* (May 1990) pp. 48-53.

Ro, Byung T. "The Disclosure of Capitalized Lease Information and Stock Prices." *Journal of Accounting Research* (Autumn 1978), pp. 315-340.

Ronen, Joshua and Ashwinpaul C. Sondhi. "Debt Capacity and Financial Contracting: Finance Subsidiaries." *Journal of*

Accounting Auditing and Finance (Spring 1989), pp. 237-265.

Rose, Peter. "Standby Letters of Credit Letters: Determinants of Their Growing and Pivotal Role in U.S. and International Banking." working paper, Texas A & M University, November,1989.

Rue, Joseph E. and David E. Tosh. "Should We Consolidate Finance Subsidiaries?" *Management Accounting* (April 1987), pp. 45-50.

Salem, George M. "Selling Commercial Loans: A Significant New Activity for Money Center Banks." *The Journal of Commercial Bank Lending* (April 1986), pp. 2-13.

Salmonson, R. F., R. H. Hermanson, and J. D. Edwards. *Accounting Principles*. Plano: Business Publications, Inc. 1983.

Schauer, Ariane. The Impact of Loan Sales on the Safety of the Banking System. dissertation, University of California, Los Angeles, 1992.

Shevlin, Terry. "Taxes and Off-Balance-Sheet Financing: Research and Development Limited Partnerships." *The Accounting Review* (July 1987), pp. 480-509.

Smith, Clifford W., Charles W. Smithson, and Lee Macdonald Wakeman. "The Market for Interest Rate Swaps." *Financial Management* (winter 1988), pp. 34-44.

Smith, Clifford W., Jr. and Jerold B. Warner. "On Financial Contracting An Analysis of Bond Covenants." *Journal of Financial Economics* 7 (June 1979), pp. 117-161.

Sondhi, A. C., D. Fried, and J. Ronen. "Finance Subsidiaries and Debt Capacity." Unpublished paper, New York University, 1988.

Sterling, Robert R. "Positive Accounting: An Assessment." *Abacus* (September 1990) pp. 97-135.

Stewart, John E. "The Challenges of Hedge Accounting." *Journal of Accountancy* (November 1989), pp. 48-56.

"Strong Senior Hiring Seen in Financial Sector." *Journal of Accountancy* (July 1987), pp. 39-42.

Thomas, Martin R. "A Theoretical and Empirical Study on the Use of Loan Sales by Financial Firms (Securitization)." Dissertation, Pennsylvania State University, 1991.

Toolan, Dennis M. "Standard Documentation Should Reduce Expenses, Control Some Risks." *Commercial Lending Review* (Fall 1991) pp. 77-79.

Turnbull, Stuart M. "Swaps: A Zero Sum Game?" *Financial Management* (Spring 1987), pp. 15-21.

Quinn, Lawrence R. "Seller Beware." *World Trade* (April 1992) pp. 110-113.

Urabel, Frank J. *The Impact of Securitization and Loan Sales on Regional Banks* dissertation, the Stonier Graduate School of Banking, 1989.

Vang, David. "Savings and Loan Capital and The Use of Interest Rate Swaps." *The American Economist* (Fall 1992) pp. 50-57.

Verkuil, Paul. "Bank Solvency and Guaranty Letters of Credit." *Stanford Law Review*. (May 1973), pp. 716-739.

Wall, Larry D. "Interest Rate Swaps In An Agency Theoretic Model With Uncertain Interest Rates." *Journal of Banking and Finance* (May 1989) pp. 261-270.

Watts, Ross L. and Jerold L. Zimmerman. *Positive Accounting Theory*. Englewood Cliffs: Prentice-Hall, Inc., 1986.

Watts, Ross L. and Jerold L. Zimmerman. "Towards a Positive Theory of the Determination of Accounting Standards." *Accounting Review* (January 1978), pp. 112-134.

"The Demand for and Supply of Accounting Theories: The Market for Excuses." *Accounting Review* (January 1978), pp. 273-305.

Whittaker, Greg. "Interest Rate Swaps: Risk and Regulation." *Economic Review*. (March 1987), pp. 3-13.

Williams, Paul F. "The Logic of Positive Accounting Research." *Accounting, Organizations & Society* (14: 1989) pp. 455-458.

Wishon, Keith and Lorin Chevalier. "Interest Rate Swaps: Your Rate or Mine?" *Journal of Accountancy* (September 1985), pp. 63-83.

Zimmer, Steven A. *Credit Risk in Interest Rate and Currency Swaps (Default Losses)* dissertation, Harvard University, 1991.

Zimmerman, Jerold L. "Taxes and Firm Size." *Journal of Accounting and Economics* (August 1983), pp. 119-149.

Zmijewski and Hagerman. "Income Strategy Approach to the Positive Theory of Accounting Standard Setting/Choice." *Journal of Accounting and Economics*. 2 (August 1981), pp. 51-63.

Index